D1285017

Dedication & Thank You

Dedicated to the one I loved and will love forever, **Bryna Solon**, my departed wife, best friend, lover, and business partner for much of our lives. I miss your presence sweetheart, but I experience you in mind and spirit every day.

I also wish to thank all of you who provided emotional and financial support during her illness, including donors, shoppers, visitors, and associates connected to the *ALS* and *MD Associations*, plus those who offered their condolences by phone, email, or in person.

Most importantly, I want to thank my sister *Elinor*, nephew *Stephen*, and brother-in-law *Dewain,* who passed away four months to the day after *Bryna*. Your support was immeasurable.

I also want to thank all of you who supported the creation of this book, contributors, editors, sounding boards, and proofreaders.

If you wish to support the ALS & MD Associations in their fight to find a cure for these debilitating diseases, go to…

https://www.gofundme.com/BrynaALSBattle
All donations go to ALS & MD

Bryna
3rd Edition Updated - 5th Printing

To order additional books, see last page.

About the Author

My name is Mel Solon, I'm 82 years young; feel 35 physically, and way smarter than I used to be in my 20s.

I've been in the motivation, personal-development field since 1971. Prior to that I was a CPA and stock-broker. After five tax seasons, I was taxed to my limits. After watching the stock-market crash during training, I began navel gazing and contemplating my future. Soon thereafter, I discovered the self-development field.

I am neither a therapist, a psychologist, nor a spiritual counsellor, though my material touches people at a very deep personal level. Instead, I'm just a really, really good organizer who has spent a lifetime collecting, organizing and sharing practical self-help knowledge through live seminars, an audio presentation and articles, my time-management system, and my two books, all organized in ways that only an anal-retentive, former CPA could imagine.

My first book, *"Quotations To Help You-From Out of Their Minds"* contains **8,540 screened quotations** of ageless wisdom, organized and indexed under **1,500 key words**. Intellectual, motivational, and therapeutic, this compendium of thought on self-development and our potential for happiness is like thousands of psychology, philosophy, and self-help books all rolled into one. I, shamelessly, call it the most extraordinarily useful and useable book of quotations that you and your mind could ever benefit from.

My second book, a relationship handbook for thinkers, entitled the *"Relationship Compatibility Checklist"* was written and published to honor **Bryna**, my departed beloved wife, best friend, and business partner for much of our lives.

Bryna passed in 2016, three weeks after our 50th anniversary, following a courageous battle with **ALS, Lou Gehrig's Disease**, a terminal, degenerative, motor-neuron illness with no current cure. Never having had kids, I was her 24-7, full-time caregiver for the last years of her life. She was my life, my motivation, and my inspiration for writing this book.

For you romantics, we met on a Friday at a **Beverly Hilton Hotel** singles dance, got engaged three days later on **Valentine's Day**, and married three weeks later in **Vegas**. We effectively dated more in those three weeks than most people do in months or even years.of dating. Mostly, we talked and talked and talked some more, about everything and anything, on occasion, from morning to morning.

— *About the Author* —

Knowing something about compatibility and the value of making a marriage work, **Bryna** and I intended to someday write a book on relationships.

Our goal — increase the happy marriage rate, reduce the divorce rate, and save people from the heartache of saying, *"If only I knew then what I know now."*

Our long career in the self-development field had reaffirmed what we had always known — at the heart of fulfilling, long-lasting relationships is kind, open. honest communication with ourselves, our partner, and close family and friends.

Although she is no longer here physically, I recently committed to fulfill our intention to write a book on relationships. The result...the *"Relationship Compatibility Checklist,"* a fun, easy to use tool designed to provoke thought and stimulate conversation about life and the dynamics of interpersonal relationships.

To learn more about both my books,
visit my website at *thethinkingplace.com.*
To purchase the *Relationship Compatibility Checklist*,
go to *Amazon.Com;* search by either *Mel Solon* or title. Enjoy!

Rodin's "The Thinker"

Written for...

**anyone making or re-evaluating
any major life-changing decision,
especially ones concerning intra- and
interpersonal relationships, such as...**

whether or not to...

- Begin or end a dating relationship
- Move in with a love interest
- Get engaged
- Get married
- Get divorced
- Pick a life or business partner
- Sign a lease with a roommate

Table of Contents (alphabetically)

Dedication & Thank You...1
About the Author 2
Table of Contents (alphabetically)..5
This book will help you in four ways:...6

1.	APPEARANCE & LOOKS	11
2.	BACKGROUND	16
3.	CHILDREN	20
4.	COMMUNICATION	25
5.	DATING	32
6.	EATING & FOOD	36
7.	EDUCATION & INTELLIGENCE	41
8.	ENTERTAINMENT & SPORTS	46
9.	HEALTH, FITNESS & MEDICAL	51
10.	LIFESTYLE ROUTINES	59
11.	LIVE-IN RELATIONSHIPS	62
12.	LOVE	67
13.	MARRIAGE	73
14.	MISCELLANEOUS	81
15.	MONEY, WORK, FINANCIAL	106
16.	PERSONALITY & CHARACTER	113
17.	PHILOSOPHY	133
18.	POLITICS & GOVERNMENT	146
19.	RELATIONSHIPS	152
20.	RELIGION	161
21.	SEX	164
22.	SOCIAL ISSUES	170
23.	TIME	175

10-Secrets To A Long & Happy Marriage 179
30 Great Quotations 180
Testimonials 183
How to Order Additional Books: 187

This book will help you in four ways:

1.   **Know thyself:**

Interview and profile yourself. Is your relationship with yourself compatible with the life you envision to live? Discover how unique you really are. Know yourself, your deal breakers, and problematic relationship issues, before deciding if you're compatible with someone else.

2.   **Rethink past relationships:**

Understand why previous relationships didn't work. Put the past to bed. Hopefully you'll never again have to say, *"If only I knew then what I know now."*

3.   **Appraise a current relationship:**

Are you truly made for each other? Are you and your partner on the same page intellectually, emotionally, psychologically, and financially regarding your attitudes about life, relationships, and your world-view? Is it time to move in, move out, or run for the hills, or time to reevaluate your compatibility, reconcile your differences, and make your relationship work even better?

4.   **Evaluate a potential relationship:**

Determine if a potential relationship is likely to succeed or not. Discover and resolve differences before taking the plunge. Could this be the love of your life? Avoid spending weeks, months, or years dating and vetting a relationship that may be doomed from the start. Don't guess, don't wonder, ask the hard penetrating questions.

—Introduction—

Relationship Compatibility Checklist

What is it?

Quite simply, it's a book of over 700 stimulating, thought-provoking questions organized under 23 categories of life. written to help you crystallize your thinking about life and how it intertwines with your relationship status. Plus it can help you find your perfect match, someone who is a good fit for your heart and mind, hopefully the love of your life. What it's not is an advice or rules book.

Because you are always in a relationship with yourself, the first step before deciding if you're compatible with someone else, is to know yourself. By answering these true-false, yes-no, multiple choice, open-ended questions, you will gain greater insight into questions like…What do you value? What are your wants and needs? What are your goals and dreams? In short, what do you want out of life and what do you want in a life partner? To help clarify your answers to these questions, use this book as an in-depth way to interview and profile yourself. As a byproduct, you'll learn just how unique you really are and why finding your soul mate can be such a challenge. With its broad perspective on life, reading this list will stimulate you to ask, is the life you're living compatible with the life you envision to live?

To truly know yourself, it's also important to rethink your past relationships. Read this book and there's a good chance you'll learn the real reason or reasons why previous relationships didn't work. With the insights gleaned from this exercise, you'll hopefully never again have to say, *"If only I knew then what I know now."*

By helping you clarify your desires and preferences related to choosing a mate or life partner, this book will increase your chances of choosing wisely. This could save you weeks, months, or even years of dating and vetting a relationship that may be doomed from the start. This is time you can never get back and could instead be better invested in finding a more compatible match. What a time saver!

— *Introduction* —

If you're already in a relationship, whether it's a challenging or loving one, this book can help you determine if you truly are made for each other. Are you and your partner on the same page psychologically, philosophically, intellectually and financially? Do you have a similar world-view? Are you compatible in all 8 areas of life: mental, physical, emotional, spiritual, social, financial, family, and career? By helping you answer these questions, this book can help you decide if it's time to move in, move out, or run for the hills? Or, is it time to re-evaluate your compatibility, reconcile your differences and make your relationship work even better?

This book works on the premise that discovering the answers to life begins with asking the right questions. The questions in this book are organized under **23 life categories**. They cover both major and minor issues that can affect the dynamics of interpersonal relationships, from whether the toilet seat should be left up or down to how to raise children. The central purpose of these questions, many controversial, is to provoke thought, stimulate conversation, and turn your thoughts into words. Note that this book doesn't tell you how to think, but rather suggests what to think about.

Keep in mind there are no absolutely right or wrong answers, just your subjective opinions expressed as a starting point for deliberation or discussion. As you've heard a thousand times, the secret to making a relationship work is communication. This book makes it easier to talk about almost anything, including sensitive topics that are often not thought or talked about until they become issues.

The message is simple, listen and talk, then talk some more. If a discussion is 'off the table,' it's already an issue. With this book you can address and resolve issues in the present, possibly months or years in advance of when they might otherwise have arisen.

While many questions are thought-provoking, others are light-hearted. This makes them perfect as conversation starters or ice-breakers for first dates.

When reviewing the questions alone, whether you're in a relationship or not, answer first for yourself, then ask yourself, how would you feel if your partner or a potential partner were to choose differently or the opposite? In answering this question, choose PC for potential conflict or DB for deal breaker. If there are no red flags, choose NI for non-issue.

— *Introduction* —

If you have difficulty choosing between true and false, yes and no, or among multiple choice answers, simply pick the answer you most lean toward. Avoid the inclination to say 'neither,' or 'it depends'   since there are always exceptions and qualifiers.

If sharing with a partner, some questions may expose areas of disagreement. When discussing your differences, I encourage you to engage your sense of humor. Treat it as a game. Do so and the entire experience can be enlightening, stimulating, and even fun. Where there are conflicts, look at them as opportunities to test your creative skills at finding compromises and resolving problems, or as a learning experience and a chance to open your mind and grow.

Whatever you feel about an entry, be careful not to underestimate the value of what may appear to be a petty or trivial issue. You'd be surprised, or maybe not, at how little it can take to start an argument. A discussion of these minor issues can sometimes be quite revelatory..

Here now are five often asked questions about using this book.

One, how do you handle answers that may not be truthful? The fact is everyone lies to some degree, by omission, exaggeration, and sometimes intent. Sometimes we do so to protect another's feelings. At other times, we do so in an attempt to think well of ourselves. The fact is, you may never know for sure if your partner is telling the truth. However, because of the comprehensiveness of this checklist, and the unique structuring of the questions, you will have a pretty good idea if your partner is being less than open and honest, or someone who, on balance, you can trust.

Two, how will you know if you and your partner are compatible? With no practical way to keep score, you will know in your gut. Your trust and confidence in your feelings will come as a byproduct of discussing and thinking clearly about such a wide breadth of issues germane to life and relationships.

Three, can you ever really know someone? Of course not, but this checklist can get you closer than you could ever imagine.

Four, what about dating websites or speed-dating events? No problem, but save your final decision until you've reviewed this book, with or without a partner.

— *Introduction* —

Five, what about 'dating-relationships' that are just for fun, sex, and companionship? My answer, enjoy them. However, partnerships, live-in relationships, and marriages have much more at stake. When these relationships fail, they can cost those involved greatly, including the financial costs of divorce - the related costs of starting over - the time wasted in dating and vetting an incompatible love interest; and the heartache and emotional turmoil often inherent in ending 'bad' relationships. If children are involved, they too will suffer. Using this book effectively can save you all three: money, time, and heartache.

In conclusion, I believe this book can help increase the happy marriage rate and decrease the divorce rate, often quoted as 50%. Note that this statistic doesn't account for relationships that would end in divorce, were it not for financial, children, or religious issues, or the insecurity of one or both partners. A decrease in the divorce rate can come about in two ways: One, by helping people make better relationship choices at the outset, and two, by helping couples bring their issues to the forefront so they can reconcile their differences and save their marriages. This can be done either on their own or with the help of a professional couples counselor. So, better safe than sorry, choose your life partner wisely.

I believe this book can also help couples who would like to get married, but hesitate to commit out of fear. By working and playing with this list, couples are better able to face and resolve, in advance, the troublesome issues that many people fight over, argue about, or get divorced over. Doing this openly and honestly in a non-defensive setting can give a hesitant couple the courage and confidence to take the plunge.

Lastly, keep in mind, life is too short to live in an incompatible relationship. You deserve better. Good luck!

At the end of the checklist, enjoy reading the 10 secrets to a long and happy marriage, and the 30 quotations on love, marriage, sex, relationships, friends, and friendship.

For more information on what Why Not? Publications is all about, visit our website, **www. thethinkingplace.com.**

1.   APPEARANCE & LOOKS

Important! Please read.

TABLE OF CONTENTS — Page 5
23 Chapters Listed Alphabetically — 723 Main Questions —
Key words in each chapter are in alphabetical order for that chapter.

ANSWER CHOICES
Y-N (Yes No) — T-F (True False) — A-B-C (Multiple Choice)

NI (Non-Issue) — PC (Potential Conflict) — DB (Deal Breaker)

HOW TO ADDRESS THE QUESTIONS
Whether you're in a relationship or not, answer first for yourself, then ask yourself, how would you feel if your partner or a potential partner were to choose differently or the opposite? If reviewing with a partner and areas of disagreement arise, engage your sense of humor, remain calm, and discuss your differences civilly.

JUDGING AN ENTRY
Whatever you feel about an entry, be careful not to underestimate the value of what may appear to be a petty or trivial issue. You'd be surprised, or maybe not, at how little it can take to start an argument or reveal a major difference of opinion. A discussion of these minor issues can sometimes be quite revelatory..

RIGHT & WRONG
There are no absolutely right or wrong answers, just your subjective opinions expressed as a starting point for deliberation or discussion.

☆☆☆☆☆

— Appearance & Looks —

1. **AGE: How old are you?** ....**NI-PC-DB**
    ➤ (How old do you feel? — Is age just a number? — When does age matter? — Does the answer depend on whether the relationship is professional, social, or romantic? — Is age a legitimate topic open for discussion? — How would you feel, what would you think, if someone seemed to be avoiding or sidestepping the age question? — Do you guess one's age, if it's not given?)

2. **AGING: How long do you want to live? — A. forever, B. as long as you're healthy, C. minimum 75, D. 75-100, E. 101+** ....**A-B-C-D-E / NI-PC-DB**
    ➤ (How well are you handling aging? — Do you think happy people live longer? — Does eating well & taking care of yourself guarantee a long life? — Does eating poorly, smoking & drinking guarantee a short life? — How much does longevity depend on luck & genetics? — How much does living a long life depend on attitude & a life-long happy marriage? — If you had only six months to live, how would you live them?)

3. **ATTRACTIVENESS: What variables affect your definition of attractiveness?** ....**NI-PC-DB**
    ➤ (symmetry — uniqueness — visage — face-shape, **i.e.,** oval — heart — triangle — upside-down-triangle — square — round — diamond — rectangular — pear — long/oblong — other attractiveness factors, **i.e.,** breast or penis size — eyes — nose — lips — jaw-line — forehead — cheekbones — smile — hair — feet & toes — ears & lobes — body shape — fitness — non-physical, **e.g.,** personality — character — comportment — demeanor — confidence — poise — temperament — spirit — Would your partner going bald be an issue? — Is it true that attractiveness is subjective & 'beauty is in the eye of the beholder'? — Are there any norms of attractiveness? — Are the eyes the windows to the soul? — How do you describe someone's eyes, e.g., big, small, round, almond, beady, droopy, sleepy, hooded, slanted, prominent, deep-set, protruding, narrow, partially closed, other? — Can the eyes alone, absent any other micro-facial expressions, reveal love, happiness, sadness, fear, disgust, anger, hate, surprise, & boredom? — Can they reveal the depth of one's true character? — How is this related to 'mind-reading'? — Do you manscape?)

— *Appearance & Looks* —

4. **ATTRACTIVENESS: Do you like the way you look, weight & attractiveness?**...........................Y-N / NI-PC-DB
    ➤ (Are you self-conscious about aspects of your body? — Do you suffer from body dysmorphia or body shaming? — Do you believe that everyone has something they're not thrilled with about their body or personal appearance, from the size or shape of their nose to their fungus toes?)

5. **BODY DESCRIPTION: How important is body description? — A. very, B. somewhat, C. not very?** ....
    ....A-B-C / NI-PC-DB
    ➤ (shape — size — height — weight — tone & fitness — Is too tall or too short a deal breaker?)

6. **BODY ENHANCEMENTS: What's your attitude toward improving your appearance?** ....NI-PC-DB
    ➤ (implants, **e.g.,** breasts — penis — booty — chin & pecs — How do you feel about, **e.g.,** — padded bras — wigs — toupees — dentures — caps — veneers — rhinoplasty — facelift — tattoos or tattoo removal — CoolSculpting or Cryoablation — liposuction — botox?)

7. **BODY HAIR: How do you feel about back, underarm & leg hair?** ....NI-PC-DB
    ➤ (Is too-hairy a dealbreaker?)

8. **CHARACTER: Can you judge a person's character by their appearance?** ....Y-N / NI-PC-DB
    ➤ (Can you tell by looking at a person, their appearance, if they're a liar, a criminal, a child molester, a domestic abuser, or, a 'good' or 'bad' person? — In short, can you tell a book by its cover?)

9. **COSMETICS: How important are cosmetics to you?** ....
    ....NI-PC-DB
    ➤ (How much time & money do you spend on cosmetics, primping, looking your best? — What's you attitude toward makeup for men?)

— Appearance & Looks —

10. **COSMETIC SURGERY: What's your attitude toward cosmetic surgery?** ....**NI-PC-DB**
➤ (elective — vanity — neurotic — corrective — botox parties)

11. **FACE HAIR: What's your attitude toward facial hair?** ....
....**NI-PC-DB**
➤ (clean shaven — beard, **e.g.,** full — goatee — stubble — mustache, **e.g.,** horseshoe — handlebar — standard — beard & mustache — mutton chops/sideburns — other — women **re:** eyebrows — peach fuzz — mustache)

12. **FASHION SENSE: Are you fashion conscious?** ....
....**NI-PC-DB**
➤ (desire & expense to be in style — designer labels — expression of yourself — vintage — suit & tie — casual chic — jeans & tee shirt — sweats — When choosing your wardrobe, which is more important, function, comfort, or style? — Do you prefer casual or formal? — Are you familiar with French Tuck?)

13. **HEAD HAIR: How important is hair style? — <u>A. very,</u> <u>B.</u> <u>somewhat,</u> <u>C.</u> not very?**...........................**A-B-C / NI-PC-DB**
➤ (long — short — cropped — wavy — curly — mohawk — crew cut — bald — shaved — bun — bouffant — bob — braids — color, **e.g.,** black — blond — red — brown — burgundy — blue — silver — salt & pepper)

14. **HYGIENE: How important is body odor? — <u>A. very,</u> <u>B.</u> <u>somewhat, C.</u> not very?**...........................**A-B-C / NI-PC-DB**
➤ (breath — body — hair — fragrance — perspiration)

15. **LANGUAGE & VOICE: How important is one's language & voice? — <u>A. very,</u> <u>B. somewhat,</u> <u>C.</u> not very?**...**A-B-C / NI-PC-DB**
➤ (accent — dialect — spoken & written language — bi-lingual — easy or difficult to understand — vulgar or tasteful — voice, **i.e.,** fast or slow — high or low — soft or loud — tone — intensity — energy level — Do you know any words or signs in ASL-American Sign Language?)

— Appearance & Looks —

16. **LOOKS: On a scale of 1 to 5, how important are looks & appearance in choosing a mate?** ....
....1-2-3-4-5 / NI-PC-DB
➤(handsome — hunky — cute — pretty — gorgeous — beautiful — attractive — rugged — nondescript — average — striking — adorable — sexy — Is there a correlation between attractiveness, success & happiness? — Were your parents attractive, in your opinion?)

17. **SKIN COLOR: How important is skin color? — A. very, B. somewhat, C. not very?** ....A-B-C / NI-PC-DB
➤ (light — fair — medium — olive — tan — brown — dark brown — black — shades thereof?)

2.   BACKGROUND

Important! Please read.

TABLE OF CONTENTS — Page 5
23 Chapters Listed Alphabetically — 723 Main Questions —
Key words in each chapter are in alphabetical order for that chapter.

ANSWER CHOICES
Y-N (Yes No) — T-F (True False) — A-B-C (Multiple Choice)
NI (Non-Issue) — PC (Potential Conflict) — DB (Deal Breaker)

HOW TO ADDRESS THE QUESTIONS
Whether you're in a relationship or not, answer first for yourself, then ask yourself, how would you feel if your partner or a potential partner were to choose differently or the opposite? If reviewing with a partner and areas of disagreement arise, engage your sense of humor, remain calm, and discuss your differences civilly.

JUDGING AN ENTRY
Whatever you feel about an entry, be careful not to underestimate the value of what may appear to be a petty or trivial issue. You'd be surprised, or maybe not, at how little it can take to start an argument or reveal a major difference of opinion. A discussion of these minor issues can sometimes be quite revelatory..

RIGHT & WRONG
There are no absolutely right or wrong answers, just your subjective opinions expressed as a starting point for deliberation or discussion.

☆☆☆☆☆

— Background —

18. **ANCESTRY: What's your ancestry/genealogy?** .NI-PC-DB

    ➤ (race — ethnicity — nationality — citizenship — heritage — DNA ancestry — DNA-genetics — Does DNA determine who you are? — Does DNA determine who or what you can become? — What does DNA determine? — Which determines your destiny & future more, your ancestral DNA history or your present choices? — In what way would knowing your ancestry DNA change your life, such as learning that you were related to George Washington, Nixon, Hitler, Hellen Keller, Mother Teressa, or Gandhi? — Have you pursued your genetic history?)

19. **BACKGROUND CHECK: How far will you go to exercise due diligence re: a potential partner's background?** ....NI-PC-DB

    ➤ (Internet searches — self-investigation — enlistment of friends & family — professional background checks **re:** employment history — drug & criminal offenses — marital history & status — domestic or child abuse — addictions — previous residence — no investigation, you'll trust your gut — etc.)

20. **CULTURAL UPBRINGING: Where were you born &/or raised?** ....NI-PC-DB

    ➤ (US, city & state — other country — small town or big city — immigrant or native born — background roots, **e.g.,** professional — business — medical — dental — legal — engineering — blue-collar — white collar — entertainment — arts — farming — government — other — Do you regularly engage in any notable traditions or customs? — Has your cultural upbringing shaped your view of how the genders are expected to relate?)

21. **EDUCATION:** (see **Education** main heading) ....NI-PC-DB

22. **FAMILY: What were your early family circumstances ....** ....NI-PC-DB

    ➤ (single or two parent home — gay parents — interracial marriage — foster home or orphanage — adopted — sperm bank baby — influence of extended family members — family size — living conditions — financial, **i.e.,** poor — middle-class — well-off — wealthy — etc.)

— Background —

23. **HOW RAISED: How were you raised?** ....**NI-PC-DB**
➤ (tough love — disciplined or lenient — control over your diet — support for or control over your teenage decisions — degree of independence — exposure to drinking & drugs — tattoos & piercings — punishment & consequences **re:** cutting school — bad grades — disrespectful behavior — attitude **re:** modesty — nudity & sex — rules **re:** use of TV — internet — phone —other — What lessons did you learn growing up about money — power — status — education — prejudice — class consciousness? — Have your attitudes & the lessons you've learned changed much over the years? — What were your nicknames? — Were you ever subjected to physical or emotional abuse as a child or teen? — Do you love your parents? — Have you forgiven your parents? — Do you believe they did the best they could in preparing you for adulthood? — Do you hold your parents or upbringing responsible for your adult problems?)

24. **HISTORY: What is your residence & car history?** ....**NI-PC-DB**

25. **PARENTS: How did your parents get along?** ....**NI-PC-DB**
➤ (Did they argue? — Did they fight like cats & dogs? — Did they hardly ever fight? — Were they both dominants or both submissive? — Was one submissive, passive & easygoing, which one? — Was one dominant, which one?)

26. **RELIGION:** (see **Religion** main heading) ....**NI-PC-DB**

— Background —

27. **VALUES: Who taught you your most important values?** ....**NI-PC-DB**

➤ (your church or religion — your parents — other family members — teachers — counsellors — therapists — recovery programs — self-help seminars — audio-video programs — near death experience — books — TV — radio.— life experience — internet — social media — ties to a group or organization — psychology or philosophy classes — best friends — other — Which values, virtues, character traits, or principles did you learn from them — which of the following words or concepts resonate with you **e.g.,** importance of words — character — leadership — tolerance — forgiveness — love — courage — charity — trustworthiness — honesty — authenticity — sincerity — integrity — frugality — self-acceptance — self-confidence — open-mindedness — commitment — flexibility — order & organization — simplicity — systemization — routine — variety — change — stimulation — gratitude — sacrifice — service — cooperation — hope — optimism — listening — science — critical thinking — common sense — intelligence — logic — responsibility — accountability — humor — patience — persistence — determination — challenge — stability — solitude — calm & peaceful — loyalty — justice — fairness — mercy — empathy — sympathy — kindness — compassion — respect for other's time & feelings — forgiveness — ethics —standing up for yourself — independence — other? — Is being responsible the same as being accountable? — How are hope & optimism different? — Ever been impatient to 'get there' or 'get started, but very patient when it came to implementation & follow through? — Regarding patience, when you're second in line at a red light & it changes to green, how long do you give the car in front of you to move, before giving them a toot? — What could a friend do to you that would be unforgivable?)

3.   CHILDREN

Important! Please read.

TABLE OF CONTENTS — Page 5

>23 Chapters Listed Alphabetically — 723 Main Questions —
>Key words in each chapter are in alphabetical order for that chapter.

ANSWER CHOICES

>Y-N (Yes No) — T-F (True False) — A-B-C (Multiple Choice)
>NI (Non-Issue) — PC (Potential Conflict) — DB (Deal Breaker)

HOW TO ADDRESS THE QUESTIONS

Whether you're in a relationship or not, answer first for yourself, then ask yourself, how would you feel if your partner or a potential partner were to choose differently or the opposite? If reviewing with a partner and areas of disagreement arise, engage your sense of humor, remain calm, and discuss your differences civilly.

JUDGING AN ENTRY

Whatever you feel about an entry, be careful not to underestimate the value of what may appear to be a petty or trivial issue. You'd be surprised, or maybe not, at how little it can take to start an argument or reveal a major difference of opinion. A discussion of these minor issues can sometimes be quite revelatory..

RIGHT & WRONG

There are no absolutely right or wrong answers, just your subjective opinions expressed as a starting point for deliberation or discussion.

✰✰✰✰✰

20 of 187

— Children —

28. **BABY/GERM PROOFING: How important is baby/germ-proofing? — A.** very, **B.** moderately, **C.** somewhat ....A-B-C / NI-PC-DB
➤ (Can too much cleanliness have a detrimental effect on a child's immune system? — How personally concerned are you with germs & cleanliness?)

29. **BABY SITTING: What's your attitude toward help with watching your children?** ....NI-PC-DB
➤ (baby sitters — nannies — family — shared responsibility — custody & visitation issues)

30. **BREAST FEEDING: What's your attitude toward breast feeding in public or in public bathrooms?** ......NI-PC-DB

31. **BULLYING: While preferring neither, would you rather that your child — A.** be bullied, **B.** be accused of being a bully? ....A-B / NI-PC-DB

32. **CHEATING: Are you aware of the cheating epidemic among tweens & teens in class & sports?** ....Y-N / NI-PC-DB
➤ (issues, **e.g.,** peer pressure —emphasis on grades vs. knowledge — need for a strong moral compass focused on integrity, values & ethics — excuse that everyone does it — technology makes it easy — Are legacy admissions to prestigious colleges a form of cheating? — Is it cheating to pay to get top recruits in college sports programs?)

33. **CIRCUMCISION: Are you — A.** for circumcision, **B.** against it? ....A-B / NI-PC-DB

34. **CONFLICTS: Are you prepared for dealing with sibling rivalries &/or step-children?** ....Y-N / NI-PC-DB

35. **DAUGHTER: Is it appropriate for a father to hug, kiss, peck on the cheek, hold hands in public with a teenage daughter?** ....Y-N / NI-PC-DB

— Children —

36. **DECISIONS: When making decisions, how important is the phrase, 'in the best interests of the child'? —** A. an important factor, B. the ultimate factor? ....
....**A-B / NI-PC-DB**
➤ (Do you support vaccinations for your child? Do you want other people's children vaccinated?

37. **DEPRESSION: Do you have experience with children's emotional issues?**......................................**Y-N / NI-PC-DB**
➤ (ADHD — autism — depression —despair — loneliness — cutting — talk of suicide — drugs — ostracism — bullying — rejection — sexuality — feeling stupid or ugly — body & hormonal changes — Can pushing kids to be involved in multiple extracurricular activities cause them stress? — Are children affected by scorekeeping in sports &/or accademics?)

38. **DESIGNER BABIES: How do you feel about the idea of genetically chosen or designer-engineered babies?**
....**Y-N / NI-PC-DB**
➤ issues **re:** ethical — medical — undesirable results — religious concerns — psychological effects on the child in later life

39. **DIAPERS: Who's responsible for changing diapers & potty training? —** A. you, B. your partner, C. both ....
....**A-B-C / NI-PC-DB**
➤ (Which do you prefer, cloth or disposable?)

40. **EMPTY NEST: How does the prospect of an empty nest make you feel?** ....**NI-PC-DB**
➤ (afraid — sad — lonely — excited —other)

41. **IMPORTANCE: How important are your children?**
....**NI-PC-DB**
➤ (Are their lives & happiness more important than your own? — Are their lives more important than that of your spouse? — In a life & death situation & you could save either your children or your spouse, how would you choose? — Would you annually acknowledge the birthday of a stillborn?)

— Children —

42. **INVOLVEMENT: How involved are you in your children's lives?** ....**NI-PC-DB**
➤ (homework — quality of their education —choice of majors — where to go to college — development of their minds — extracurricular activities — special classes like music, dance or art — parent-teacher meetings — getting to know their friends — quality time — Is the degree of participation in your children's lives an issue? — Are you still learning, growing & developing your mind?)

43. **KIDS: Do you — A.** love kids, **B.** not crazy about them? ...
....**A-B / NI-PC-DB**
➤ (Do you want or not want kids? — how many — gender preference — combined families — sharing parental responsibilities — for or against birth-control or a vasectomy — Are you open to adoption, foster-care, a surrogate, Big Brother/Sister programs or artificial insemination if unable to conceive? — Do you believe the study that claims 40% of all births in the US are out of wedlock?)

44. **PARENTHOOD: How fulfilling is or do you imagine motherhood or fatherhood to be? — A.** extremely, **B.** very, **C.** moderately.................................**A-B-C / NI-PC-DB**
➤ (Is being a stay-at-home parent a joy or a job?)

45. **PREGNANCY: Does the idea of pregnancy engender — A.** feelings of joy, **B.** anticipation of difficulties & complications?...**A-B / NI-PC-DB**
➤ (What's your attitude toward drinking, smoking, drugs & nutrition during pregnancy?)

46. **SAFETY: When driving with them, do you implement child safety rules consistently?** ....**Y-N / NI-PC-DB**
➤ (child car seats — seat belts — working air bags — seating in front or back seat — Is it safe to leave young children in a car on a cool day for a short time? — Are you comfortable discussing inappropriate touching with your children?)

23 of 187

— Children —

47. **RAISING: What are your child rearing principles?** ....
....**NI-PC-DB**

   ➤ (**re:** tough love — disciplined or lenient — religion — control of
   child's diet — support for or control over teenager's decisions —
   tattoos & piercings — drinking & drugs — degree of independence
   — hours to be home — homework — dress code — punishment &
   consequences **re:** cutting school — bad grades — cheating —
   shoplifting — bullying — or disrespectful behavior — amount of
   allowance — is an allowance a right or does it need to be earned —
   attitude **re:** modesty, nudity & sex — rules **re:** use of TV, internet &
   phone — rule about when to leave or get up from the dinner table
   — beliefs **re:** Santa Clause, tooth fairy, etc.)

48. **SAYING NO: Does wanting to be a friend to your child
   cause internal conflict when having to say 'no' as a
   parent?** ....**Y-N / NI-PC-DB**

49. **SCHOOL DISTRICT: How important is the reputation of
   your school district? — A.** very, **B.** moderately, **C.**
   somewhat, **D.** not at all..........................**A-B-C-D / NI-PC-DB**
   ➤ (Do you want your children to learn cursive?)

50. **SENSITIVITY: How sensitive are children to the quality
   of their parents' emotional relationship? — A.** very,
   B. more than parents realize, **C.** hardly at all ....
   ....**A-B-C / NI-PC-DB**
   ➤ (Can children sense their parents' anger — love — passive-
   aggressiveness — resentment — happiness — etc.? — Can the
   child's sensitivity affect their own behavior? — How sensitive are
   children to favoritism? — Is showing favoritism normal, or to be
   avoided as much as humanly possible.)

4. COMMUNICATION

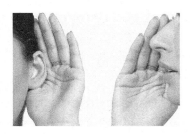

Important! Please read.

TABLE OF CONTENTS — Page 5

23 Chapters Listed Alphabetically — 723 Main Questions —
Key words in each chapter are in alphabetical order for that chapter.

ANSWER CHOICES

Y-N (Yes No) — T-F (True False) — A-B-C (Multiple Choice)
NI (Non-Issue) — PC (Potential Conflict) — DB (Deal Breaker)

HOW TO ADDRESS THE QUESTIONS

Whether you're in a relationship or not, answer first for yourself, then ask yourself, how would you feel if your partner or a potential partner were to choose differently or the opposite? If reviewing with a partner and areas of disagreement arise, engage your sense of humor, remain calm, and discuss your differences civilly.

JUDGING AN ENTRY

Whatever you feel about an entry, be careful not to underestimate the value of what may appear to be a petty or trivial issue. You'd be surprised, or maybe not, at how little it can take to start an argument or reveal a major difference of opinion. A discussion of these minor issues can sometimes be quite revelatory..

RIGHT & WRONG

There are no absolutely right or wrong answers, just your subjective opinions expressed as a starting point for deliberation or discussion.

— Communication —

51. **AGREEMENT: Do you find the phrase, 'let's just agree to disagree' — A.** a way to reduce tension, **B.** a ploy to avoid further discussion, **C.** an acknowledgement that the parties to a quarrel tolerate but don't accept the opposing position ....**A-B-C / NI-PC-DB**

52. **ARGUMENTS: Most arguments are about details, variables, context, degree, tone & words more than principles or facts.** ....**T-F / NI-PC-DB**
➤ (What percent of arguments do you think are about control?)

53. **ARGUMENTS: Arguments & conflict are common & practically unavoidable in intimate relationships.** ....
....**T-F / NI-PC-DB**
➤ (If true, can this be attributed to differences in our perspectives & frames of reference, the by-product of our inherent & developmental uniqueness?)

54. **ARGUMENTS: In an argument, is the statement, "I don't want to talk about it" — A.** acceptable, **B.** frustrating, **C.** unacceptable? ....**A-B-C / NI-PC-DB**
➤ (When confronting an obvious problem, how would you respond to the words, "Drop it, leave me alone, there's nothing wrong, I'm fine"? — Which is more productive - attacking, acting out, or talking?)

55. **ARGUMENTS: In an argument, what would your reaction be to the statement, "that's true, you're absolutely right"? — A.** you'd calm down, **B.** you'd be surprised, confused, **C.**you'd be suspicious......................
....**A-B-C / NI-PC-DB**

56. **ARGUMENTS: In an argument, is your goal — A. win-win, B. a 'zero-sum-win-lose outcome'?** .**A-B / NI-PC-DB**

26 of 187

— Communication —

57. **CONFLICT: Do you agree that when you know you are loved & lovable, you are better able to communicate, tolerate & discuss conflicting issues than when such assurance is lacking?** ....Y-N / NI-PC-DB
➤ (How skilled are you at conflict resolution? — Is it ever productive to unilaterally walk away from a conflict because it's stressful? — Does the concept of MAD - mutually assured destruction have a place in conflict resolution?)

58. **CONFLICT: Do you consider yourself tolerant of conflict?** ....Y-N / NI-PC-DB
➤ (Are you able to tolerate contentious, heated debates, without resorting to ultimatums & name-calling? — Can you handle, **e.g.,** venting — raised voices — yelling — arguing — debating — bickering — being interrupted without emotionally reacting by, **e.g.,** withdrawing — leaving the premises — threatening divorce — breaking things — becoming passive-aggressive — sarcastic — resorting to domestic or 'intimate-partner-violence'—IPV? — Does your tolerance for conflict depend on how secure you are in the relationship? — What distinguishes an intense & passionate argument from one labeled angry & hostile?)

59. **CONTROVERSY: When confronted with a controversial point of view, are you inclined to — A. agree with the speaker, B. share a contrary or opposing view, C. propose a balanced position, D. decline or avoid giving any opinion or feedback at all, E. ask questions & seek more information before responding?** ....
....A-B-C-D E / NI-PC-DB
➤ (Does your answer depend on your relationship to the speaker? — Does it depend on the strength of your commitment to your position or point of view? — Do you consider yourself argumentative? — Do you tend to avoid confrontation? — Do you have the attitude that there are three sides to every story, theirs, yours & the truth? — When you disagree with someone do you attack the person, their character, or their ideas? — Have you ever been accused of not fighting fair?)

— Communication —

60. **FIGHTING: What are some euphemisms & other words for 'fighting'?** ....NI-PC-DB
➤ (quibbling — bickering — bantering — quarreling — arguing — debating — spats — squabbles — disputes — disagreements — communication breakdowns — shouting match — verbal & physical altercations — raised voices — assault — abuse —What kind of arguments lead to the worst fights: arguments over styles & boundaries, over the details & specifics of an issue, or discussions of character flaws? — In an argument, which is more important to you, being right or being happy?)

61. **FIGHTING: The secret to repairing relationship problems is talking, listening, apologizing & forgiving.** ....T-F / NI-PC-DB
➤ (Do you find it easy or difficult to apologize? — How do you feel about people who say 'never apologize'? — Is going to bed 'mad' productive or counter productive?)

62. **FIGHTING: Why do some couples claim they never fight?** — **A.** if they do fight, they claim they don't in order to protect their image as a couple, **B.** they don't fight because one or both partners are too insecure to stand up for themselves, **C.** they're anti-confrontational, venting, raised voices & yelling are off-the-table, **D.** their roles are separate & clearly defined, reducing opportunities to disagree, **E.** they have no issues where differences of opinion are consequential, **F.** they're skilled at communicating & expressing themselves, **G.** they're emotionally mature & self-controlled, **H.** their love is miraculous ....A-B-C-D-E-F-G-H / NI-PC-DB

— *Communication* —

63. **IMPORTANCE: How important are communication skills?** ....**NI-PC-DB**
➤ (verbal & non-verbal — email & texting — phone & returning calls — finding time to listen attentively — public speaking ability — sales ability — openness to discussing anything — Which is more important in social communications, being interesting or being interested? — Is the silent treatment an effective way to communicate? — When you are upset, annoyed, or pissed with someone, is it best to address the issue in the present, when the offense is taking place, or sit on it until the issue is easier to deal with?)

64. **INARGUABLE: Nothing in life is certain, absolute or inarguable.** ....**T-F / NI-PC-DB**
➤ (Can you make a philosophical statement about life that can't be challenged with the phrase, 'not necessarily' or 'it depends'? How about 'out of sight out of mind' vs. 'absence makes the heart grow fonder'? — How often has your point of view been changed with the introduction of just one new piece of contradictory or conflicting information? — Is the phrase, 'you can't change the past' debatable? — Do you agree that in response to almost anything you can say or do, there will always be someone who will call it stupid, crazy, dumb, uncool, thoughtless or unintelligent?)

65. **INTERRUPTING: Is interrupting or interjecting while someone is talking ever justified?** ....**Y-N / NI-PC-DB**
➤ (Do any of the following situations ever justify interrupting, **e.g.,** the speaker makes an untrue statement or misstatement of fact — makes a point irrelevant to the topic at hand — is filibustering or monopolizing the conversation — is repeating themselves — is sharing more information than wanted or needed — doesn't breathe or allow room for mitigating interjections — if insulted or unjustifiably accused — to clarify a misunderstanding in order to better follow the conversation — to cut off a sarcastic rant or demeaning put-down — to ask for a needed piece of information — to shorten the conversation because you need to leave or make an important call — other? — Do you agree that interrupting to change the subject or stop the flow of conversation is different than interjecting to enhance the dialog?)

— Communication —

66. **METAPHORS: Does the use of metaphors, similes, analogies & allegories — A.** always help to improve communications, **B.** sometimes get in the way of actual facts & critical thinking? ....**A-B / NI-PC-DB**

67. **PAINFUL: Which is more painful — A.** not communicating & instead walking on eggshells, stewing, biting your tongue & repressing your feelings, **B.** confrontation & venting, with open, honest communication, even if uncomfortable? ......**A-B / NI-PC-DB**

68. **PARTNER: How would you characterize your communications with your partner?** ....**NI-PC-DB**
   ➤ (incredibly open & honest — comfortable talking about feelings — no limits to what you can talk about — includes philosophical & psychological topics — stimulating — informative — supportive — usually talk about the same topics — somewhat shallow — one-sided — boring — inattentive — impersonal — argumentative — opportunities to talk are highly dependent on timing & time availability)

69. **TOGETHER: Is there any greater obstacle to 'working-well-together' than poor communication?** ....
   ....**Y-N / NI-PC-DB**
   ➤ (Is it true that people can accomplish almost anything, if they communicate well & work together as a team?)

— *Communication* —

70. **WORDS: What are 'words' & how important is your choice of words when communicating & expressing yourself?** — **A.** critically important, **B.** very important, **C.** not as important as body language, **D.** not as important as tone...**A-B-C-D / NI-PC-DB**
➤ (Is the following definition of words meaningful? — "Words are tools & symbols of language used to communicate our thoughts, feelings & mental pictures." — Is the following definition of communication useful? — Communication is a common union between you & I leading to action. — Are relationships damaged more often by hurtful words, or by disturbing behavior & actions? — How do the following words affect communication: — you always, you never — judgmental comments beginning with you're too this or too that? — Have you ever argued about the difference between facts & opinions, facts & the truth, facts & feelings, or interjecting vs. interrupting?)

5. DATING

Important! Please read.

TABLE OF CONTENTS — Page 5

    23 Chapters Listed Alphabetically — 723 Main Questions —

Key words in each chapter are in alphabetical order for that chapter.

ANSWER CHOICES

    Y-N (Yes No) — T-F (True False) — A-B-C (Multiple Choice)

    NI (Non-Issue) — PC (Potential Conflict) — DB (Deal Breaker)

HOW TO ADDRESS THE QUESTIONS

Whether you're in a relationship or not, answer first for yourself, then ask yourself, how would you feel if your partner or a potential partner were to choose differently or the opposite? If reviewing with a partner and areas of disagreement arise, engage your sense of humor, remain calm, and discuss your differences civilly.

JUDGING AN ENTRY

Whatever you feel about an entry, be careful not to underestimate the value of what may appear to be a petty or trivial issue. You'd be surprised, or maybe not, at how little it can take to start an argument or reveal a major difference of opinion. A discussion of these minor issues can sometimes be quite revelatory..

RIGHT & WRONG

There are no absolutely right or wrong answers, just your subjective opinions expressed as a starting point for deliberation or discussion.

☆☆☆☆☆

— Dating —

71. **BASKETS: Would having your eggs in more than one basket give you emotional security & reduce your chances of feeling jealous?** ....Y-N / NI-PC-DB
➤ (How can you feel emotionally secure & not prone to jealousy in a committed relationship? — Can you explain the difference between jealousy & envy?

72. **DATE: What makes a date?** ....NI-PC-DB
➤ (hanging out — coffee — dinner — movies — a concert — a kiss — sex — Does who pays matter? — Does a promise to call matter? — Are alcohol, drugs & date rape a concern? — How many dates does it take to get past the "best behavior" obstacle to really knowing someone?)

73. **DATING: What's the least amount of time you would date someone before you would take your relationship up a notch or to the next level?** ....
....NI-PC-DB

74. **DEFINITION: How do you define your dating-courting relationship?** ....NI-PC-DB
➤ (casual — good friends — more than friends — no strings attached — going steady — hanging out — soul mate — the love of your life — friends with benefits — boyfriend/girlfriend — lovers — serious — committed — exclusive — fiancee' — affair with or as an adulterer or adulteress — blind date — mixed signals — exclusive without sex — like — really like — fond of — crazy about — have feelings for —care about — reason for living — always thinking about — makes life worth living — never felt like this before)

75. **DISTANCE: Is you relationship — A. geographically desirable, B. not?** ....A-B / NI-PC-DB
➤ (long-distance dating — cyber-chatting — email — webcam — instant-messaging — letter writing — texting — sexting — Zoom — Skype — FaceTime — other)

— Dating —

76. **PARENTS: Have you met your partner's parents?**
....**Y-N / NI-PC-DB**
➤ (Do you feel accepted by them?)

77. **PURPOSE: What's your purpose for dating?** ....**NI-PC-DB**
➤ (regular sex — booty calls — fun — time structuring — an adventure — to learn about each other as you go — to find the love of your life — to find a long-term loving relationship — to find a marriage partner — to test intellectual & psychological compatibility — friendship — companionship — to find a playmate)

78. **QUALITIES: What other qualities besides smart, funny, rich, good looking & good kisser are you looking for in a date or mate?** (see **Personality** main heading) ....**NI-PC-DB**

79. **THE CHASE: What makes the thrill of the chase sometimes more satisfying than the catch? — A.** attitude, **B.** chemicals & hormones, **C.** the game of 'hard to get'** ....**A-B-C / NI-PC-DB**

80. **UNDATABLE: What makes someone undateable or become undateable?** ....**NI-PC-DB**
➤ (your dog clearly doesn't like them — smokes — drinks — sloppy, ungroomed & unkempt — bad breath — picks their nose — lies — broke — has kids — doesn't like kids — negative attitude — has no ambition — no car — not punctual — parks with an illegal placard in a handicapped space — they're married —they don't want to get married — marriage is their highest priority — they're rude to waitstaff — other)

— *Dating* —

81. **WHERE TO FIND: Where can you find a dating prospect?** ....**NI-PC-DB**
➤ (online kitten & catphishing — cooking classes — speed dating events — dances — bars — grocery stores — singles clubs — church groups — community or neighborhood meetings — friends & family fix-ups — school — work — beach — dating services — singles personal ads — book-store readings — other — Are you able to approach & engage an attractive stranger in intelligent conversation about relationships? — The book can help.)

See also Live-in, Love, Marriage, Sex, Relationships, Communications main headings.

6. EATING & FOOD

Important! Please read.

TABLE OF CONTENTS — Page 5

23 Chapters Listed Alphabetically — 723 Main Questions —

Key words in each chapter are in alphabetical order for that chapter.

ANSWER CHOICES

Y-N (Yes No) — T-F (True False) — A-B-C (Multiple Choice)

NI (Non-Issue) — PC (Potential Conflict) — DB (Deal Breaker)

HOW TO ADDRESS THE QUESTIONS

Whether you're in a relationship or not, answer first for yourself, then ask yourself, how would you feel if your partner or a potential partner were to choose differently or the opposite? If reviewing with a partner and areas of disagreement arise, engage your sense of humor, remain calm, and discuss your differences civilly.

JUDGING AN ENTRY

Whatever you feel about an entry, be careful not to underestimate the value of what may appear to be a petty or trivial issue. You'd be surprised, or maybe not, at how little it can take to start an argument or reveal a major difference of opinion. A discussion of these minor issues can sometimes be quite revelatory..

RIGHT & WRONG

There are no absolutely right or wrong answers, just your subjective opinions expressed as a starting point for deliberation or discussion.

☆☆☆☆☆

— Eating & Food —

82. **BEVERAGES: What are your beverage preferences?** ....
....**NI-PC-DB**

➤ (coffee or tea — diet or regular sodas — tonic water — plain club soda — fruit or vegetable juice — tap, bottled or coconut water — shakes — milk, **e.g.,** almond — whole — coconut — or low-fat — protein drinks — Gatorade — wine — beer — alcohol — other — Do you use sweeteners like stevia & Splenda? — Does not getting your coffee when you want it affect your mood? — How important to taste is the year, vineyard, & cost of wine?)

83. **CONDIMENTS: What do you put on hot dogs vs. hamburgers?** ....**NI-PC-DB**

➤ (ketchup — mustard — mayonnaise — relish — thousand-island dressing — other)

84. **COOKING: Are you a good cook?** ....**Y-N / NI-PC-DB**

➤ (Have you ever had food poisoning?)

85. **COOKING: Is it inhumane to drop lobsters into boiling water?** ....**Y-N / NI-PC-DB**

86. **CLEANUP: Which approach do you prefer to doing dishes? — A.** pre-soak, **B.** wash as soon as you're done eating, **C.** leave them in the sink till you're ready, **D.** use the dishwasher, **E.** leave them for the housekeeper, **F.** leave them for the kids, **G.** other ....
....**A-B-C-D-E-F-G / NI-PC-DB**

➤ (Do you put quality knives in the dishwasher? — Are you particularly fastidious about keeping the kitchen clean?)

87. **CUISINE: What are your cuisine preferences?** ..**NI-PC-DB**

➤ (Italian — Chinese — Mexican — Spanish — American — Indian — Persian — Thai — Greek — Korean — Vietnamese — German — cajun — sushi — soul — deli — mediterranean — international buffet — fast food — frozen dinners — vegan — etc.)

— Eating & Food —

88. **DIET: How would you label your diet?** ....**NI-PC-DB**

➤ (high or low fat — high or low carb — low sugar — low calorie — low sodium — high or low protein — Paleo — South Beach — Weight Watchers — Mediterranean — Mayo Clinic — Atkins — Nutri-System — vegetarianism — vegan — animal based — plant based — balanced — Purium —healthy — unhealthy — eclectic — flexible — other — Have you ever sought advice from a nutritionist? — Do you ever fast?)

89. **EATING: What are your attitudes & preferences re: eating?** ....**NI-PC-DB**

➤ (cooking in — ordering in — eating out — take-out — fast food — restaurants with atmosphere — self-serve restaurants — buffets — pubs — Which of your preferences do you do most often? — How do you feel about, **e.g.,** eating in bed — eating food that fell on the floor — the importance of breakfast — eating standing up? — How many meals do you eat each day? — How religiously do you adhere to expiration dates on food?)

90. **EATING: Do you have a problem with anorexia or bulimia?** ....**Y-N / NI-PC-DB**

91. **EATING: Do you — A. eat to live, B. live to eat?**...............
....**A-B / NI-PC-DB**

➤ (Is eating an important daily activity? — What's your attitude toward speed & communication during meals? — Do you eat or snack throughout the day? — Is cooking a major part of your life? — Are you offended if your cooking isn't appreciated?)

92. **FOOD: Certain foods should not touch each other on a plate, e.g., gravy.** ....**T-F / NI-PC-DB**

➤ (Do you combine foods in individual bites?)

— Eating & Food —

93. **FOOD: What are your attitudes & preferences re: food?** ....**NI-PC-DB**
    ➤ (Are you nutritionally aware? — Do you read labels? — Do you eat frozen dinners? — Is food cost an issue? — Are calories an issue? — Is organic or GMO an issue? — Which of the following do you prefer, **e.g.,** fish — red meat — pork — turkey — poultry — pasta — fruits & vegetables — soups — pizza & burgers — oysters — snails — egg style? — Are there foods you hate? — Do you avoid processed foods? — Do you eat hot dogs? — Do you eat bread crust?)

94. **FOOD: What is your attitude toward countries that eat cats &/or dogs?** ....**NI-PC-DB**
    ➤ (What do Americans eat that some people keep as pets?)

95. **FRUITS: What are your fruit preferences?**.........**NI-PC-DB**
    ➤ (bananas — oranges — apples — kiwis — limes — lemons — grapefruits — pears — tangerines — plums — nectarines — peaches — berries — cantaloupe — watermelon — cherries — avocados — tomatoes — grapes — coconut — pineapple — mangos — mandarins — other)

96. **HUNGER: Does being hungry trigger or cause you to be irritable & angry (hangry)?**...................**Y-N / NI-PC-DB**

97. **OVEREATING: Beyond misreading hunger cues, do you generally overeat because you're — A. stressed B. angry, C. anxious, D. excited, E. depressed, F. lonely, G. bored, H. craving a taste, I. longing for a particular food, J. driven by a habit, K. encouraged by another person, L. hormones, M. any or all of the above?** ....
    ....**A-B-C-D-E-F-G-H-I-J-K-L-M / NI-PC-DB**
    ➤ (How do you approach food at social events?)

98. **SALAD DRESSINGS: What are your salad dressing preferences?** ....**NI-PC-DB**
    ➤ (French — Thousand island — Ranch — Blue cheese — Italian — Vinegar & oil — Fat-free — Home-made — Goddess — other)

— Eating & Food —

99. **SHARING: What's your attitude toward sharing food off of your's or another's plate?** ....NI-PC-DB

100. **SHOPPING: What are your shopping preferences?** ....
....**NI-PC-DB**
➤ (wholesale clubs — specialty stores — farmers' markets — small neighborhood grocery stores — traditional supermarkets — whole food markets — alone or with a partner — Internet — by phone & delivery — Costco — Amazon — other)

101. **TREATS: What are your treat or snacking preferences?** ....**NI-PC-DB**
➤ (popcorn — potato chips — candy — chocolate — ice cream — cake — pies —brownies — muffin tops — cookies, **e.g.,** Oreos — chocolate chip — oatmeal — peanut butter — other)

102. **VEGETABLES: What are your vegetable preferences?** .
....**NI-PC-DB**
➤ (lettuce — asparagus — broccoli — Brussels sprouts — carrots — potatoes — rice — peas — string beans — corn — cauliflower — peppers — kale — onions — turnips — beets — cabbage — mushrooms — spinach — artichokes —okra — squash — cucumbers — other)

103. **VITAMINS & SUPPLEMENTS: Do you take vitamins &/ or supplements?** ....**Y-N / NI-PC-DB**
➤ (for brain health — increased sexual performance — specific ailments — general health — apple cider vinegar — CQ10 — glucosamine/chondroitin — turmeric — probiotics — multi-vitamin — vitamin E — vitamin B12 — Prevagen — other — Which is more important to the effective use of your brain: your diet, the quality of your brain's content (information & knowledge), or knowing how to think, clearly, calmly, rationally, goal-directedly, & optimistically, especially in a crisis.)

7. EDUCATION & INTELLIGENCE

Important! Please read.

TABLE OF CONTENTS — Page 5
23 Chapters Listed Alphabetically — 723 Main Questions —

Key words in each chapter are in alphabetical order for that chapter.

ANSWER CHOICES
Y-N (Yes No) — T-F (True False) — A-B-C (Multiple Choice)

NI (Non-Issue) — PC (Potential Conflict) — DB (Deal Breaker)

HOW TO ADDRESS THE QUESTIONS
Whether you're in a relationship or not, answer first for yourself, then ask yourself, how would you feel if your partner or a potential partner were to choose differently or the opposite? If reviewing with a partner and areas of disagreement arise, engage your sense of humor, remain calm, and discuss your differences civilly.

JUDGING AN ENTRY
Whatever you feel about an entry, be careful not to underestimate the value of what may appear to be a petty or trivial issue. You'd be surprised, or maybe not, at how little it can take to start an argument or reveal a major difference of opinion. A discussion of these minor issues can sometimes be quite revelatory..

RIGHT & WRONG
There are no absolutely right or wrong answers, just your subjective opinions expressed as a starting point for deliberation or discussion.

☆☆☆☆☆

— Education & Intelligence —

104. **BACKGROUND: What's your educational background?** — **A.** high school, **B.** college, **C.** graduate school, **D.** professional degree(s), **E.** trade or technical school, **F.** online courses, **G.** school of hard knocks, **H.** self-taught or home-schooled....**A-B-C-D-E-F G H / NI-PC-DB**
➤ (Are your junior high, high school, & teenage memories positive, negative, or unremarkable?)

105. **BRAIN: Do you consider yourself more of a** — **A.** right brain, creative thinker, **B.** left brain, analytical thinker, **C.** equal?..**A-B-C / NI-PC-DB**
➤ (Do you agree with these premises of NLP (Neural Linguistic Programming): when our eyes look to the right, we may be in a creative thinking mode, possibly creating a deception, & when looking to the left, we may be trying to remember recorded information? — When explaining events & happenings relative to cause & effect, do you generally look for simple explanations & single causes, or do you try to identify multiple variables as percentages of the overall cause? — Are you familiar with Occam's razor, the problem-solving principle of parsimony? It essentially states that simpler solutions are more likely to be correct than complex ones. In other words, 'keep it simple stupid.' — Are you an 'out-of-the-box' thinker? — Who is smarter, men or women?)

106. **BUSINESS EDUCATION: What's your level of business acumen?**..**NI-PC-DB**
➤ (basic math **re:** calculating estimates, percentages & interest — creating budgets — reading & writing contracts — evaluating decision-making support data — knowledge of the Uniform Commercial Code — bookkeeping skills — maintaining documentation & receipts — getting hiring references — knowledge of basic accounting principles — ability to read & prepare simple financial statements — knowledge of taxes — fixed & variable costs — knowledge of metrics **re:** conversions for body height & weight & temperature, Fahrenheit-Celsius)

— Education & Intelligence —

107. **CONTINUING EDUCATION: Do you have an interest in continuing education?** ....Y-N / NI-PC-DB
➤ (current plans — academic pursuits — formal — informal — How do you feel about teachers protesting for wages & funding? — Are you familiar with 'first-generation, low-income scholarships' at highly selective universities?)

108. **EMOTIONAL & SOCIAL INTELLIGENCE: Do you consider yourself emotionally & socially intelligent?**
....Y-N / NI-PC-DB
➤ (self-awareness — self-mastery — self-control — healthy self-esteem — introspective & reflective vs. shallow & superficial — Can you talk about feelings? — Are you open to criticism, forgiveness & apologizing? — Are you sensitive to other's feelings & emotional states of mind? — Do you know the difference between empathy & sympathy?)

109. **HISTORY: Are you a history buff?**...............Y-N / NI-PC-DB
➤ (world — U.S. — European — mid-eastern — modern — ancient — prehistoric — military — religion — other)

110. **IGNORANCE: Ignorance is bliss.**.................T-F / NI-PC-DB
➤ (When did you first hear this? — Who told you?)

111. **INFORMAL: What's the source of your informal education?** ....NI-PC-DB
➤ (friends — books — magazines — newspapers — newsletters — talk radio — audio & video programs — internet — blogs — TV — podcasts — smartphone — etc.)

112. **MATH-ABILITY: How are you at math? — A. good, B. fair, C. poor** ....A-B-C / NI-PC-DB
➤ (skill or comfort talking with & using numbers — calculating, **e.g.,** percentages — tips — return on investments — interest expense on large purchase — measurements in food recipes — pricing food values — making change — etc.)

— Education & Intelligence —

113. SALES TRAINING: Have you had any sales training? ...
....Y-N / NI-PC-DB

➤ (classes — seminars — books — audio & video programs — on-the-job experience)

114. SMARTS: Do you consider yourself smart? ....
....Y-N / NI-PC-DB

➤ (Do you have street smarts? — Do you have common sense? — Are you witty? — What's your IQ? — Are you cerebral? — Are you a critical vs. non-critical thinker? — Do you make wise decisions? — Do you believe all decisions require trade-offs? — Do you agree with the quote that, "To know that you know what you know & to know that you don't know what you don't know, this is intelligence?" — Is knowing what not to believe a sign of intelligence? — In which areas of life is decision-making most troublesome: mental, physical, emotional, spiritual, social, financial, family & career? — Do you consider yourself average or above average intelligence? — Do you agree with the statement that everyone is smarter than we think they are?)

115. STEM EDUCATION: Do you have a desire to improve your STEM education? ....Y-N / NI-PC-DB

➤ (Science — Technology — Engineering & Math — Do you believe it should include Art?)

116. TECHNOLOGY: Are you computer literate? — A. very, B. moderately, C. slightly D. hardly ......A-B-C-D / NI-PC-DB

➤ (How proficient or comfortable are you **re:** the Internet — computers — laptops — tablets — cellphones — YouTube — Google — apps — email — texting — Amazon — Facebook — Linkedin — Twitter — Flickr — Instagram — SnapChat — Tinder — Pinterest — Kindle — etc.? — Are you addicted to the Internet, Facebook, Twitter, or Instagram or your phone?

— Education & Intelligence —

117. TECHNOLOGY: How aware are you of computer jargon? — A. very, B. somewhat, C. a little, D. hardly.....
....A-B-C-D / NI-PC-DB

➤ (brain-hacking — data-mining of micro expressions — phishing — cookies — browsing-history privacy — viruses — ransomeware — spam — malware — hacking — dark web — GPS tracking — anti-virus software — mixed reality technology — holograms & speech technology — RAM & ROM — USB — bots & trolls — hardware — software — hash tags — Should law enforcement have access to encryption key codes to unlock cell phones? — Do you know how to disappear & become a ghost to digital technology? — Are you a social media widow or widower?)

118. TECHNOLOGY: How involved are you with technology? — A. very, B. somewhat, C. a little, D. hardly ....A-B-C-D / NI-PC-DB

➤ (How much time are you involved with technology per day? — How much time do you spend on Facebook or playing games? — Is your involvement for business, personal, or both? — How expensive is your involvement **re:** hardware — software — service contracts & the value of your time? — Does your partner have access to your passwords? — Do you need help when tech problems arise? — Do you ever voluntarily disconnect from your electronic yokes? — Are you a PC or Mac person? — Do you use earbuds or keep your phone away from your ear to avoid radiation & brain cancer?)

8. ENTERTAINMENT & SPORTS

Important! Please read.

TABLE OF CONTENTS — Page 5

23 Chapters Listed Alphabetically — 723 Main Questions —
Key words in each chapter are in alphabetical order for that chapter.

ANSWER CHOICES

Y-N (Yes No) — T-F (True False) — A-B-C (Multiple Choice)
NI (Non-Issue) — PC (Potential Conflict) — DB (Deal Breaker)

HOW TO ADDRESS THE QUESTIONS

Whether you're in a relationship or not, answer first for yourself, then ask yourself, how would you feel if your partner or a potential partner were to choose differently or the opposite? If reviewing with a partner and areas of disagreement arise, engage your sense of humor, remain calm, and discuss your differences civilly.

JUDGING AN ENTRY

Whatever you feel about an entry, be careful not to underestimate the value of what may appear to be a petty or trivial issue. You'd be surprised, or maybe not, at how little it can take to start an argument or reveal a major difference of opinion. A discussion of these minor issues can sometimes be quite revelatory..

RIGHT & WRONG

There are no absolutely right or wrong answers, just your subjective opinions expressed as a starting point for deliberation or discussion.

☆☆☆☆☆

— Entertainment & Sports —

119. **AWARD SHOWS: Are you a fan of award shows?** ....
....**Y-N / NI-PC-DB**
➤ (Academy — Golden Globes — People's Choice — Grammy's
Billboard — Tony's — MTV — ACM — BET — etc.)

120. **DANCING: How important is dancing to your lifestyle?**
....**NI-PC-DB**
➤ (How often do you go? — Are you good at it? — Have you ever
taken lessons? — Do you watch *Dancing With The Stars*?)

121. **ENTERTAINMENT: In what entertainment categories or
activities do you spend most of your leisure time?** ....
....**NI-PC-DB**
➤ (How do you spend your time when not working? — How would
you spend it if money & time were no object, **e.g.,** TV — movies —
music — talk-radio — reading — sports — exercise — drinking —
eating — drugs — socializing — partying — sex — hobbies —
traveling — social media — surfing online — gaming — family —
church or charitable activities — shopping — other? — How do you
feel about boxing & mixed martial arts as entertainment? — Do you
read the comics or graphic novels? — Which affects your
entertainment enjoyment more, what you're doing or whom you're
doing it with? — Do you ever listen to radio stations with views
contrary to yours?)

122. **HOLIDAYS & VACATIONS: How important are holidays
& vacations to your lifestyle?** — <u>A. very, B.
somewhat, C. not very</u> ....**A-B-C / NI-PC-DB**
➤ (cruises — staycations — weekend trips — travel — getting away
from it all — timeshare — resorts — etc.)

— Entertainment & Sports —

123. MOVIES: How do you watch movies? ....NI-PC-DB

➤ (DVR — computer — tablet — cellphone — in theaters — on TV — DVDs — Netflix — Amazon — Hulu, etc. — Google — Apple — What's your attitude toward talking or whispering during TV programs or movies, in your own home with your partner, with guests, or in theaters? — Do you binge watch? — What's your attitude toward commercials & closed captions? — Are you emotionally repulsed by some commercials? — Do you like or avoid trailers? — In a theater, do you prefer sitting close to the front, the middle or up top? — Do you ever go to the movies alone? — How often do you go out to the movies?)

124. MOVIES: What are your movie preferences? ....NI-PC-DB

➤ (action — horror — drama — adventure — comedies — biopics — teen & preteen life — animation — period historic — romance — chick flicks — survival against all odds — tear-jerkers — revenge themes — science fiction — monsters — heroes — catastrophes — spy-intrigue — political thrillers & suspense — fantasy — time travel — feel good — educational — faith-based dramas — psycho-dramas — heroes in jeopardy or peril — porn — love stories, **e.g.,** When Harry Met Sally — Love Story — The Notebook — Titanic — Pretty Woman — Brokeback Mountain — Sleepless In Seattle — Gone With The Wind — Romeo & Juliet — etc. — franchises, **e.g.,** Star Wars — Harry Potter — Lord of the Rings — Fast & Furious — Toy Story — James Bond — Batman — Superman — Star Trek — Spider Man — X-Men — Mission Impossible — Madagascar — Iron Man — Pirates of the Caribbean — Transformers — Despicable Me — Jurassic Park — Ice Age — Indiana Jones — Kung Fu Panda — Marvel — etc. — Have you ever seen the same movie more than twice? — How important to you is it to have similar movie preferences with a partner? — Have you ever gone to the movies with someone other than your partner? — What percent of your movie choices are to please your children, your partner, or a friend? — Do you ever see movies after reading the book?)

— Entertainment & Sports —

125. **MUSIC: What are your music preferences?**.......**NI-PC-DB**
➤ (old — new — contemporary — classical — popular — hard or
soft rock — rap — hip-hop — jazz — blues — bluegrass — R & B
— country — big band — Reggae — Latin — heavy metal — show
tunes — grunge — punk — funk —other — How important to you is
it to have similar music preferences with a partner? — Are you an
audiophile? — How loud to you like your music? — Which is more
important to you, the music, the lyrics, or equal?)

126. **OUT OF HOME: What are your out of home
entertainment preferences?** ....**NI-PC-DB**
➤ (bars & happy hours — movies — parties — live theater —
concerts — miniature golf — walking on beach — picnics —
amusement parks — visiting friends — sports — etc.)

127. **READING: Do you consider yourself a reader?**.............
....**NI-PC-DB**
➤ (fiction — nonfiction — novels — crime — murder mysteries —
history — romance — westerns — science — educational — poetry
— career related — etc. — Would you ever read the last chapter of
a mystery novel before reading the book? — Have you ever reread
a novel?)

128. **SPORTS: Which sports or athletic activities interest
you the most?** ....**NI-PC-DB**
➤ (team or individual — active or spectator — football — baseball
— basketball — hockey — tennis — golf — skiing — soccer —
bowling — bicycling — rollerskating — surfing — racquet or
handball — volleyball — sailing — shooting range — badminton —
other — level of intensity — how often — how expensive)

129. **TALK RADIO: Do you listen to talk radio on any basis
of regularity?** ....**Y-N / NI-PC-DB**
➤ (for entertainment — topical or political news — food for thought
— conservative or liberal stations — entertainment & sports news)

— *Entertainment & Sports* —

130. TV: What are your TV habits? ....NI-PC-DB
➤ (When do you do most of your TV viewing? — number of hours per day — channel surfing — control of the remote — background while working — recording for later viewing — Do you watch reruns, **e.g.**, intentionally, by accident, or when nothing new is on? — Do you watch TV in the bedroom?)

131. TV: What are your TV program preferences? ....NI-PC-DB
➤ (news — medical — legal — police/cop/crime — political — reality — game shows — sports — soaps — action — movies — sitcoms — dramedies — teen-life — talk shows — investigative — entertainment news — historic specials — educational — programs on how to survive — nature — science — food shows — home improvement programs — travel — mini-series — late night — series or episodic — daytime — evening — weekends — cable — satellite — little TV — America's Favorite Home Videos — Ridiculousness — Big Bang — Law & Order — Game of Thrones — other)

132. VIDEO GAMES: Are you into video games? — A. very, B. somewhat, C. no interest ....A-B-C / NI-PC-DB
➤ (Are you judgmental of people who play them for hours on end? — Do you play with people you've never met? — Do you play with people from other countries?)

133. WHITEWASHING: Does whitewashing in Hollywood disturb you? ....Y-N / NI-PC-DB

9. HEALTH, FITNESS & MEDICAL

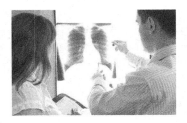 

Important! Please read.

TABLE OF CONTENTS — Page 5

23 Chapters Listed Alphabetically — 723 Main Questions —

Key words in each chapter are in alphabetical order for that chapter.

ANSWER CHOICES

Y-N (Yes No) — T-F (True False) — A-B-C (Multiple Choice)

NI (Non-Issue) — PC (Potential Conflict) — DB (Deal Breaker)

HOW TO ADDRESS THE QUESTIONS

Whether you're in a relationship or not, answer first for yourself, then ask yourself, how would you feel if your partner or a potential partner were to choose differently or the opposite? If reviewing with a partner and areas of disagreement arise, engage your sense of humor, remain calm, and discuss your differences civilly.

JUDGING AN ENTRY

Whatever you feel about an entry, be careful not to underestimate the value of what may appear to be a petty or trivial issue. You'd be surprised, or maybe not, at how little it can take to start an argument or reveal a major difference of opinion. A discussion of these minor issues can sometimes be quite revelatory..

RIGHT & WRONG

There are no absolutely right or wrong answers, just your subjective opinions expressed as a starting point for deliberation or discussion.

☆☆☆☆☆

— Health, Fitness & Medical —

134. **ALLERGIES & SENSITIVITIES: Do any of the following affect you negatively?** ....Y-N / NI-PC-DB
➤ (cats — sight of blood & guts — gluten — dairy — lactose — soy — nuts — scents & smells — cigarette or cigar smoke — ant & roach sprays — fragrances — bleach & other cleaning products — seasonal allergens — germs — dust — pollen — Are you concerned with germs on railings, menus, pens, or restroom faucets?)

135. **ALZHEIMER'S & DEMENTIA: Can any of the following cure or prevent Alzheimers or dementia?** ....
....Y-N / NI-PC-DB
➤ (brain diets — brain games — drugs — cognitive training exercises — vitamins — supplements — meds — Can the progression of these diseases be slowed?)

136. **ATTITUDE: Do you believe attitude (positive or negative) can affect surgical outcomes?**
....Y-N / NI-PC-DB
➤ (Do you believe attitude is a choice? — Do you believe it's possible to be happy even while ill or dying of a terminal disease?)

137. **CAREGIVING: What's your attitude toward caregiving for a spouse — an aged or ill parent — a child — a stranger as a job?** ....NI-PC-DB
➤ (Would your attitude toward caregiving depend on any of the following, **e.g.,** your financial situation — other demands on your time — closeness to the patient — availability of other caregivers, family, or friends? —Can you imagine having your or your spouse's aging parent or parents living with you? — Do you have any current caregiving responsibilities? — Is there anyone in your life whose death would change the trajectory of your life? — Would their age at the time of their death affect your answer?)

— Health, Fitness & Medical —

138. **DISABILITIES: Do you or any loved ones have any disabilities or incapacities?** ....Y-N / NI-PC-DB
➤ (How would you respond to your partner or child suddenly losing a limb or becoming blind or deaf? — How would you respond to learning that you, your mate, or child was diagnosed with a terminal illness? — Are you personally concerned about the possibility of becoming disabled & requiring full-time health-care? — Are you concerned about the cost & quality **re:** healthcare — home-care — or institutional care? — Are you concerned about needing family support or becoming a medical burden? — Do you worry about needing a hip or knee replacement? — Have you ever had a discussion about a DNR (do not resuscitate)?)

139. **DREAMS: There is nothing more important to mental health than having dreams & hope.**...........T-F /NI-PC-DB
➤ (Does it matter if the dreams are unrealistic or delusional? — Is giving false hope cruel? — What's the difference between hope & optimism, faith & belief?)

140. **DRINKING: What's your attitude toward drinking?** ....
.... NI-PC-DB
➤ (social — alcoholism — at home — in public — driving under the influence — abstinence — AA — MAD — therapy — penalties — binge — under-age — drinking age — legal blood alcohol level)

141. **DRINKING: Which of the following are most often cited for developing a drinking problem?** ....NI-PC-DB
➤ (stress & depression related to problems **re:** money — a relationship — health — work — dashed dreams — lack of meaning & purpose — loneliness — lost love — genetic predisposition — byproduct of frequency — other — Is earning another's trust sufficient motivation to give up drinking?)

— Health, Fitness & Medical —

142. DRUGS: What's your attitude toward drugs? ....NI-PC-DB
➤ (hard — recreational — prescriptive — cost — insurance — frequency — access by young people — addiction — treatment — penalties — legalization — opioid crisis — ecstasy — heroin — methamphetamines — cocaine — steroids — nicotine — hallucinogens — marijuana — vaping — e-cigarettes — CBD — Does cannabis make people more creative or are creative people drawn to cannabis? — clinical trials — foreign sources — drug interactions & side effects — warning labels — motivation of pharmaceutical companies — FDA — advice from pharmacies & pharmacists — generic vs. brands — knock-offs & fakes — other — To what degree do you believe in the placebo effect?)

143. EXERCISE & FITNESS: Are you involved in an exercise or fitness program?....................Y-N / NI-PC-DB
➤ (gym — home equipment — classes — how often — kind — intensity — session length — walking — jogging — bicycling — roller blading or ice skating — trampoline — triathlete — ultra-marathons — etc.)

144. GENITALS: Are you openly willing to discuss your experience with herpes, fever blisters, cold sores, UTIs & genital warts? ....Y-N / NI-PC-DB

145. GERMAPHOBE: Are you preoccupied with germs & cleanliness? ....Y-N / NI-PC-DB

— Health, Fitness & Medical —

146. **GUILT & REGRET: Is your mental or emotional health affected by guilt &/or regret?**...................Y-N / NI-PC-DB
➤ (Can guilt & regret serve a productive purpose? — When do guilt & regret become self-defeating? — When examining guilt & regret, do you accept that that causation & the assignment of fault, blame & responsibility can be complicated. This is due to the fact every event, while preceded by a proximate cause, was itself preceded by another antecedent, in short, another intervening cause in the chain of events. How far back, then, does blame, responsibility, and accountability go? — Who is the arbiter of blame, accountability & responsibility & to what end? — How many life-changing decisions would you like to undo? — How many things have you said that you wish you hadn't? — Have you made any major decisions you regret re: relationships, cars, jobs, careers, where to live, investments, politics, vacations, residences?)

147. **HEALTH: Health is more important than wealth.**............
....T-F / NI-PC-DB

148. **HEALTH: Which of the following is most responsible for your state of health? — A. diet & nutrition, B. exercise & physical activity, C. attitude, D. stress, E. meaning & purpose, F. environment, e.g., air & water quality, G. habits related to smoking, drinking & drugs, H. genetics?** ....A-B-C-D-E-F-G-H / NI-PC-DB

149. **HEALTHCARE: Are you preoccupied with healthcare quality & insurance?**................................Y-N / NI-PC-DB
➤ (have — don't have — want — cost & affordability — self-insurance — medications — equipment — supplies — Obamacare/ACA — Medicare — Medi-Cal — Medicaid — vaccines — Trump Care — single payer system — universal coverage — preexisting illnesses — mandate that everyone has insurance — In the phrase 'the right to life, liberty & the pursuit of happiness,' do the words 'right to life' include the right to a healthy life?)

150. **ILLNESS: Are happy people less likely than unhappy people to develop a physical illness?**......Y-N / NI-PC-DB

— Health, Fitness & Medical —

151. **ILLNESSES & DISEASES: Are you or anyone close to you affected by any of the following illnesses or concerns?** ....**Y-N / NI-PC-DB**
➤ (heart — kidney — liver — gallbladder — pancreases — Crohn's or colitis — diabetes — shingles — thyroid — ALS — MS — MD — Parkinson's — cancer — Alzheimer's — IBS — RA — COPD — PTSD — Lupus — migraines — alcoholism — fibromyalgia — Epstein-Barr — drug addiction — eczema — psoriasis — hyperhidrosis — tinnitus — Coronavirus-19? — other — How open are you to sharing your medical issues? — Wanting neither, would you rather be diagnosed with Alzheimer's or ALS? — Have you heard of a diabetes domino donor? — Would you give a family member a kidney if asked?))

152. **MEDICATIONS: Does your medical history include any long-term use of medications, including those taken over long periods during childhood?** ....**Y-N / NI-PC-DB**

153. **MENTAL HEALTH: Are you or a loved one affected by any of the following issues?** ....**Y-N / NI-PC-DB**
➤ (bipolar-manic-depression — OCD-obsessive-compulsive disorders — disruptive idiosyncratic behaviors — Asperger's syndrome — Tourettes — schizophrenia — clinical depression — chronic or free-floating generalized anxiety — suicide concerns — mentally unstable — hypochondria — self-medication with, **e.g.**, Prozac — Xanax — Zoloft — Lorazepam — or over-the-counter medications — therapy — other — In your opinion, is a main cause of suicide the feeling that one has nothing left to lose? — In your opinion, is a main cause of depression the inability to construct a future? — Do you agree that talk-therapy is the best first line intervention for dealing with suicide ideation?)

— Health, Fitness & Medical —

154. **MENTAL HEALTH: What's your attitude toward people who avail themselves of counseling or therapy? —** A. positive, B. negative, C. neutral ....**A-B-C / NI-PC-DB**
➤ (When having marriage problems, is couple counseling always an option? — Is 'happy wife, happy life' true? — Is there truth in the phrase, you're only as sick as your secrets?)

155. **MENTAL HEALTH: Most people wake up in the morning anxious & fearful about their future?** ....
....**T-F / NI-PC-DB**

156. **STOOL HEALTH: How comfortable are you discussing stool health? —** A. very, B. somewhat, C. not at all ....
....**A-B-C / NI-PC-DB**
➤ (constipation — diarrhea — color — smell — shape — size — soft — hard — frequency — diet related — medication side effects — hemorrhoids — Are you aware of what stool health can teach you about your overall health? — How open are you to discussing your medical history with a partner?)

157. **SUICIDE: How do you feel about suicide as a solution to depression? —** A. not an option, B. thought about it, C. faked it for attention ....**A-B-C / NI-PC-DB**
➤ (why suicide, **e.g.**, nothing to live for — nothing to look forward to — unrelenting physical or psychic pain — unabating depression — feeling lonely & unloved — feeling hopeless, out of options — loss of faith in God — loss of faith in oneself — loss of a love interest or a loved one — financially impoverished — death of a child — no one to talk to who cares & will listen — Have you heard the quote, "Suicide is a permanent solution to a temporary problem?" — Are you aware that suicide is most common among teens, veterans, the LGBTQ+ community, the elderly & trauma survivors?)

— Health, Fitness & Medical —

158. **SUICIDE: What are the alternatives besides suicide when feeling hopeless, at your wits end, or at the end of your rope?** ....NI-PC-DB
➤ (seek professional counseling — talk to a close friend or family member — talk to a rabbi, priest, pastor, preacher, or clergy — read or listen to positive, motivational materials — turn to your faith — hope & pray — read from the bible — if domestic abuse, remove yourself from the situation — if financially destitute, research government assistance — consider bankruptcy — consider online fundraising — research government assistance — if medical, pursue medical advice — if a criminal matter, get legal advice — consider witness protection — ask yourself, are things hopeless or just very challenging — don't dwell on resolving the whole problem, just focus on your next step — don't drink or resort to drugs unless prescribed — seek charitable resources — call the suicide hotline)

159. **TREATMENTS: How open are you to the following medical treatments?** ....NI-PC-DB
➤ (stem cells — life support — tracheotomy — feeding tubes — pacemaker — dialysis — chemotherapy — bone marrow transplants — organ transplants — alternative medicine — homeopathy — screenings — knee & hip replacements — prosthetics — How familiar are you with CRISPR & alteration of DNA to cure or prevent genetic diseases? — Are you an organ donor? — Are you afraid of doctors, dentists & needles to the extent of avoiding them even when in need of their services?)

160. **WEIGHT CONTROL: At what point would weight gain in yourself or a parter become a problem?** ....NI-PC-DB
➤ (clothes don't fit — BMI — health issues — appearance — physical limitations — effect on employment opportunities — seating on airplanes or in theaters — other)

161. **WEIGHT CONTROL: How should unhealthy weight gain in a partner be handled?** ....NI-PC-DB
➤ (with encouragement — nagging & scolding — threats & ultimatums — care & compassion — anger & resentment — diet — exercise — medication — supplements — therapy — etc.)

10. LIFESTYLE ROUTINES

Important! Please read.

TABLE OF CONTENTS — Page 5

23 Chapters Listed Alphabetically — 723 Main Questions —

Key words in each chapter are in alphabetical order for that chapter.

ANSWER CHOICES

Y-N (Yes No) — T-F (True False) — A-B-C (Multiple Choice)

NI (Non-Issue) — PC (Potential Conflict) — DB (Deal Breaker)

HOW TO ADDRESS THE QUESTIONS

Whether you're in a relationship or not, answer first for yourself, then ask yourself, how would you feel if your partner or a potential partner were to choose differently or the opposite? If reviewing with a partner and areas of disagreement arise, engage your sense of humor, remain calm, and discuss your differences civilly.

JUDGING AN ENTRY

Whatever you feel about an entry, be careful not to underestimate the value of what may appear to be a petty or trivial issue. You'd be surprised, or maybe not, at how little it can take to start an argument or reveal a major difference of opinion. A discussion of these minor issues can sometimes be quite revelatory..

RIGHT & WRONG

There are no absolutely right or wrong answers, just your subjective opinions expressed as a starting point for deliberation or discussion.

— Lifestyle Routines —

162. BATHROOM: What's your shower or tub routine? ....
....**NI-PC-DB**

➤ (morning or evening — at home — at the gym — at work — daily or less than daily — long or short sessions — functional or for pleasure — with partner, sometimes or never)

163. EATING: (see **Eating & Food** main heading) ....**NI-PC-DB**

164. EXERCISING: (see **Exercise** under **Health, Fitness & Medical**
main heading) ....**NI-PC-DB**

165. HOBBIES: Do you have any hobbies?...........................
....**Y-N / NI-PC-DB**

➤ (woodworking — artisan crafts — jewelry — needlecraft — fishing — stamps — coins — ant farm — painting — photography — quilting — gardening — other — level of involvement **re:** cost — supplies — time invested — Is your hobby marketable?)

166. PARTYING: Do you party? — A. often, B. occasionally, C. rarely, D. never ....**A-B-C-D / NI-PC-DB**

➤ (Are drugs & alcohol involved? — Do you host parties, **e.g.,** small dinner parties or large parties? — Are you invited to parties often occasionally or rarely? — Do your family members host parties?)

167. SLEEPING: Is getting a good night's sleep — A. a major issue, B. sometimes a problem, C. rarely an issue? ....**A-B-C / NI-PC-DB**

➤ (circadian rhythm — biological sleep cycle — early bird or night owl — short or long sleep cycle — light or heavy sleeper — bathroom interrupted — consequences of sleep deprivation — counting sheep — use of sleep aids — Is getting out of bed in the morning, generally speaking, easy or hard?)

168. TV: (see **TV** under **Entertainment & Sports** main heading) ....
.... **NI-PC-DB**

— Lifestyle Routines —

169. **WEEKENDS: How do you typically spend your weekends or days off?**......................................**NI-PC-DB**
➤ (time with friends & family — shopping & errands — spiritual programs — maintenance — caregiving — doing nothing — sports — exercise — catching up on work — pursuit of hobbies or crafts — sharing a hobby — no distinction between weekdays & weekends — other)

170. **WORK:** (see **Money, Work & Financial** main heading) ...**NI-PC-DB**

11. <u>LIVE-IN RELATIONSHIPS</u>

<u>*Important! Please read.*</u>

<u>TABLE OF CONTENTS</u> — Page 5
23 Chapters Listed Alphabetically — 723 Main Questions —
Key words in each chapter are in alphabetical order for that chapter.

<u>ANSWER CHOICES</u>
Y-N (Yes No) — T-F (True False) — A-B-C (Multiple Choice)
NI (Non-Issue) — PC (Potential Conflict) — DB (Deal Breaker)

<u>HOW TO ADDRESS THE QUESTIONS</u>
Whether you're in a relationship or not, answer first for yourself, then ask yourself, how would you feel if your partner or a potential partner were to choose differently or the opposite? If reviewing with a partner and areas of disagreement arise, engage your sense of humor, remain calm, and discuss your differences civilly.

<u>JUDGING AN ENTRY</u>
Whatever you feel about an entry, be careful not to underestimate the value of what may appear to be a petty or trivial issue. You'd be surprised, or maybe not, at how little it can take to start an argument or reveal a major difference of opinion. A discussion of these minor issues can sometimes be quite revelatory..

<u>RIGHT & WRONG</u>
There are no absolutely right or wrong answers, just your subjective opinions expressed as a starting point for deliberation or discussion.

☆☆☆☆☆

171. **BATHROOM: Do you keep the door open or closed when doing your business?** ....**NI-PC-DB**
➤ (Do you run water in the bathroom to hide the sound of peeing? — Do you have or want double sinks or separate bathrooms? — Would you ever share a toothbrush or razor?)

172. **BED: What are your bed preferences?** ....**NI-PC-DB**
➤ (twin — queen — king — separate — adjustable — mattress firmness — foam — age of mattress — amount of covers — electric blanket — quilt — comforter — water bed — sleep-side — bed height — sleeping bag — separate rooms)

173. **BEDROOM LIGHTING: What are your bedroom lighting preferences?** ....**NI-PC-DB**
➤ (ambient — natural — curtains — nightlight — black shades — candles — dim)

174. **CHORES: On the subject of chores & housekeeping, how do you feel about the idea, 'each according to his or her ability, each according to his or her need'?**
....**NI-PC-DB**
➤ (yard work — auto maintenance — kitchen — bathrooms — living room — offices — patios & decks)

175. **DROP-IN VISITORS: How do you handle drop-in visitors? — A. allow anytime, B. must call first, C. depends on who** ....**A-B-C / NI-PC-DB**

176. **DECORATING: Who makes the decorating decisions? — A. you, B. your partner, C. equally, D. both** ....
....**A-B-C-D / NI-PC-DB**
➤ (paint colors — furniture — wall-coverings — flooring — appliances — window coverings — over-all appearance of living spaces)

— Live-in Relationships—

177. **EXPENSES: How should the expenses of food — utilities — rent — mortgage be handled? — A.** shared equally, **B.** allocated based on income, **C.** unequally depending on the expense, **D.** depends on the commitment level of the partners, **E.** depends on who owns the home ....**A-B-C D E / NI-PC-DB**
➤ (Are money problems more common in live-in relationships, in marriage, or the same?)

178. **FLATULENCE: What's your attitude toward farting?** .....
....**NI-PC-DB**
➤ (allowed in bed — bathroom only — outside — not in same room as partner — uncontrollable — no limits — gross — natural — common sense courtesy)

179. **FLOSSING: Do you have rules governing flossing or using toothpicks?** ....**Y-N / NI-PC-DB**
➤ (Have you ever heard of a gold toothpick?)

180. **KITCHEN: Who's the cook, who cleans? — A.** you, **B.** your partner, **C.** both.................................**A-B-C / NI-PC-DB**

181. **LAUNDRY: Who does the laundry? — A.** you, **B.** your partner, **C.** both ....**A-B-C / NI-PC-DB**

182. **MARRIAGE: Is living together without being married an option?** ....**NI-PC-DB**

183. **MAINTENANCE: Are you handy when it comes to home repairs & maintenance?**....................................**Y-N**
➤ (Are you more likely to hire help or do it yourself?)

184. **PESTS: How do you react to mice, crawling insects, e.g., roaches, ants, spiders, etc.?** ....**NI-PC-DB**

— Live-in Relationships —

185. **RESIDENCE: Where do you want to live?** ....NI-PC-DB
➤ (country — U.S. city & state — beach — mountains — desert — small town — suburb — big city — climate, **e.g.,** warm — cold — temperate — tropical — four seasons — other — Is your decision affected by any of the following, **e.g.,** traffic — air quality — cost of living — wages — job opportunities — culture — taxes — weather or likelihood of hurricanes, tornadoes, or earthquakes, etc — distance from family or friends — Does hot weather make you grouchy? — Does living in a 5-star hotel intrigue you?)

186. **SHEETS: How often should they be changed?** ....
....NI-PC-DB

187. **SLEEPING: Do you have insomnia?** ....Y-N / NI-PC-DB

188. **SLEEPWALKING: Do you sleepwalk?** ....Y-N / NI-PC-DB
➤ (treatments — danger — frequency)

189. **SNORING: Do you snore?** ....Y-N / NI-PC-DB
➤ (occasionally or habitually — soft or loud)

190. **SPACE: How is space allocated?** ....NI-PC-DB
➤ (drawers — cabinets — closets — refrigerator — garage — etc. — Is storage space an issue?)

191. **TEMPERATURE: What are your temperature preferences?** ....NI-PC-DB
➤ (Do you generally prefer windows open or closed — heat on or off — air-conditioning on or off — thermostat set to warm or cool? — How affected are your preferences by seasonal changes?)

192. **TOILET: What are your toilet fixture preferences?** ....
....NI-PC-DB
➤ (bidet — seat, **i.e.,** wood — plastic — or padded — quiet flush — low flow — power flush — seat left up or down)

193. **TOILET PAPER: Should the toilet paper unroll — A. over the top, B. from the bottom?** ....A-B / NI-PC-DB
➤ (Do people with cats have a reason to choose **B**?)

— Live-in Relationships—

194. TOOTHPASTE: What are your toothpaste preferences? ....NI-PC-DB
➤ (cap kept on or off, open closed — tube smoothed out or left clumpy — separate or shared tube)

195. TRASH CANS: Should indoor trash cans be— A. covered B. uncovered? ....A-B / NI-PC-DB

196. TV & SOCIAL MEDIA: What are your TV & social-media rules in the bedroom? ....NI-PC-DB
➤ (allowed or not allowed — Is the TV allowed on while the other is sleeping? — How about earplugs or headphones? — Is TV volume or closed captioning potential issues?)

197. UTENSILS, POTS & PANS: Do you have — A. separate utensils, pots & pans, B. a common set? ....NI-PC-DB
➤ (Does the answer depend on the commitment level of your relationship? — Is a commitment ceremony the same level of commitment as a marriage?)

See also Dating, Love, Marriage, Sex, Relationships, Communications main headings.

12. LOVE

Important! Please read.

TABLE OF CONTENTS — Page 5
**23 Chapters Listed Alphabetically — 723 Main Questions —
Key words in each chapter are in alphabetical order for that chapter.**

ANSWER CHOICES
**Y-N (Yes No) — T-F (True False) — A-B-C (Multiple Choice)
NI (Non-Issue) — PC (Potential Conflict) — DB (Deal Breaker)**

HOW TO ADDRESS THE QUESTIONS
Whether you're in a relationship or not, answer first for yourself, then ask yourself, how would you feel if your partner or a potential partner were to choose differently or the opposite? If reviewing with a partner and areas of disagreement arise, engage your sense of humor, remain calm, and discuss your differences civilly.

JUDGING AN ENTRY
Whatever you feel about an entry, be careful not to underestimate the value of what may appear to be a petty or trivial issue. You'd be surprised, or maybe not, at how little it can take to start an argument or reveal a major difference of opinion. A discussion of these minor issues can sometimes be quite revelatory..

RIGHT & WRONG
There are no absolutely right or wrong answers, just your subjective opinions expressed as a starting point for deliberation or discussion.

☆☆☆☆☆

— Love —

198. **AFFECTION: How do you feel about demonstrations of love & affection in public or private?** ....NI-PC-DB
➤ (touchy-feely — hand-holding — hugging — kissing — words — poetry — cuddling — walking with arms around waist or shoulder — babying, **i.e.,** feeding — grooming — baby talk — other. — How often do you expect signs of affection, physical, or verbal? — How do you feel about pet names?)

199. **CHOICE: Is loving someone a choice?** ....Y-N / NI-PC-DB

200. **CHOICE: When you're hurting, do you want — A. empathy, B. sympathy?** ....A-B / NI-PC-DB

201. **CHOICE: Would you rather be — A. wanted, B. needed?** ....A-B / NI-PC-DB

202. **CHOICE: You can't choose whom you'll fall in love with.** ....T-F / NI-PC-DB

203. **COMPANION: Can a companion be a substitute for a love interest?** ....Y-N / NI-PC-DB

204. **CONFLICT: Can love survive if partners have strong opposing political &/or religious views?** ....
....Y-N / NI-PC-DB

205. **DECISION MAKING: Does being in love impair rational decision making?** ....Y-N / NI-PC-DB

206. **DIE FIRST: If you & the love of your life knew that at some unknown future date you were going to die a year apart, who would you prefer to go first? — A. you, B. your partner?** ....A-B / NI-PC-DB

— Love —

207. **FIRST SIGHT: Is love at first sight — A.** real & true, **B.** lustful, **C.** physical attraction, **D.** a movie fantasy, **E.** a function of pheromones, **F.** infatuation? ....
....A-B-C-D-E-F / NI-PC-DB
➤ (Are there degrees of love? — What does the deepest form of love entail?)

208. **GUARANTEE: Is having a complementary, compatible relationship synonymous with love?** ....Y-N / NI-PC-DB

209. **HAPPINESS: How important to happiness is having a life partner or love interest? — A.** very, **B.** moderately, **C.** somewhat, **D.** not necessary ....A-B-C-D / NI-PC-DB
➤ (someone to laugh & hang with — someone you can count on in good times & bad — someone who will back you up & be there for you even in conflicts with family & friends — someone who would know & care whether you've arrived home safely for the evening — someone who would support you & give you the benefit of the doubt if your character or behavior were attacked — someone to watch TV & movies with — someone to share comics with — someone who cares about the details of your life — someone who believes in you —Does your partner make you feel safe?)

210. **HEART: The heart wants what it wants.** ......T-F / NI-PC-DB

211. **INTIMACY: How do you define intimacy?** ....NI-PC-DB

212. **JEALOUSY: When you know that you are loved & lovable, you are less likely to experience or display jealousy.** ....T-F / NI-PC-DB

213. **JEALOUSY: Is jealously proof of love?** ......Y-N / NI-PC-DB

214. **LOVE: When you know you're loved, you become bolder & more self-confident.** ....T-F / NI-PC-DB

215. **LOVE: Can you love more than one person at a time?**
....Y-N / NI-PC-DB

— *Love* —

216. **LOVE: Can you make someone love you?** ....
....Y-N / NI-PC-DB

217. **LOVE: Love conquers all.** ....T-F / NI-PC-DB

218. **LOVE: Love is blind.** ....T-F / NI-PC-DB

219. **LOVE: Which is more desirable — A. perfect love, B. perfect health?** ....A-B / NI-PC-DB

220. **LOVE: Can you love someone you don't respect & admire?** ....Y-N / NI-PC-DB
    ➤ (Which is more important to you, being loved or being respected?)

221. **LOVE: How many shots does anyone get at finding true love? — A. one, B. few, C. many** .....A-B-C / NI-PC-DB
    ➤ (Does your answer depend on your age? — If widowed, are you ever too old to love again?)

222. **LOVE: Which of the following would you be willing to give up, risk the loss of, or sacrifice in the name of love — A. your life, B. your career, C. a kidney, D. your freedom, E. your friends or family, F. your integrity or reputation, G. your religion, H. your eyesight, I. your financial security, J. any or all the above** ....
    ....A-B-C-E-F G-H I-J / NI-PC-DB
    ➤ (Does your answer depend on how long you've been in love? — Does it depend on your age? — Is risking your life with the possibility of dying the same as saving the other's life knowing your own death is certain? — Is this question too depressing to ponder? — Between the love of your life & the career of your dreams, which one comes first when having to choose? — Would you follow him or her anywhere? — Is a sacrifice that is made willingly, freely & happily truly a sacrifice?)

— Love —

223. **LOVE: Is there anything we desire more than to love & be loved?** ....Y-N / NI-PC-DB
➤ (How is 'love ya, love you & I love you' different from 'I'm in love with you?' — Can tone change the meaning of the words? — Is love sometimes not enough to make a relationship last?)

224. **PRINCIPLES: Would you stand on your principles if doing so would be seen as disloyal to a loved one?** ..
....Y-N / NI-PC-DB

225. **PROOF: What is proof of true love?** ....NI-PC-DB
➤ (Can love exist without passion?)

226. **RESOLUTION: Any incompatibility issue can be resolved by partners who truly love each other.** ....
....T-F / NI-PC-DB

227. **TRUST: Can you love someone you don't trust?** ....
....Y-N / NI-PC-DB
➤ (Among fidelity, loyalty, love & trust, how do these words differ in meaning? — If you could be either trusted or loved, which would you choose? — Is it fair to state that trusting someone suggests that one believes beyond a reasonable doubt that the stated motives, intentions, or reasons behind another's words, actions or behavior embody honesty, sincerity & truthfulness — can you trust someone who is not transparent — have you heard of the concept of radical honesty & authenticity? — Which character trait elicits more trust, someone considered clever or some one labeled resourceful? — Can anyone be happy living under a cloud of suspicion?)

228. **UNCONDITIONAL: Does unconditional love have any limits?** ....Y-N / NI-PC-DB
➤ (Is an abusive, alcohol partner lovable?)

— Love —

229. WORDS: What do the words, "I love you" mean? ....
....NI-PC-DB
➤ (Does the meaning change when speaking of family, friends, a date, a spouse, pets, a car, a movie, your job, money? — What do the words, "I really like you or care about you a lot" mean? — How would you respond if you expressed your deep feelings to another & got no response?)

230. WORDS: If in a loving relationship, how frequently do you expect to hear the words "I love you"? ...NI-PC-DB
➤ (Are there any words you'd like to hear more than "I love you"?)

231. WORDS: Are the words, "If I can't have you, no one can" flattering? ....Y-N / NI-PC-DB
➤ (Are the following words evidence of true love, **e.g.,** "without you my life has no meaning," "you are my everything," "I am nothing without you"?)

See also Dating, Live-in, Marriage Sex, Relationships, Communications

13. <u>MARRIAGE</u>

<u>Important! Please read.</u>

<u>TABLE OF CONTENTS — Page 5</u>

23 Chapters Listed Alphabetically — 723 Main Questions —
Key words in each chapter are in alphabetical order for that chapter.

<u>ANSWER CHOICES</u>

Y-N (Yes No) — T-F (True False) — A-B-C (Multiple Choice)
NI (Non-Issue) — PC (Potential Conflict) — DB (Deal Breaker)

<u>HOW TO ADDRESS THE QUESTIONS</u>

Whether you're in a relationship or not, answer first for yourself, then ask yourself, how would you feel if your partner or a potential partner were to choose differently or the opposite? If reviewing with a partner and areas of disagreement arise, engage your sense of humor, remain calm, and discuss your differences civilly.

<u>JUDGING AN ENTRY</u>

Whatever you feel about an entry, be careful not to underestimate the value of what may appear to be a petty or trivial issue. You'd be surprised, or maybe not, at how little it can take to start an argument or reveal a major difference of opinion. A discussion of these minor issues can sometimes be quite revelatory..

<u>RIGHT & WRONG</u>

There are no absolutely right or wrong answers, just your subjective opinions expressed as a starting point for deliberation or discussion.

☆☆☆☆☆

— Marriage —

232. **ABUSE: Whether abuse is physical or emotional, it's unacceptable & always grounds for divorce.**...............
....T-F / NI-PC-DB

233. **AGE: Does age matter?**.............................Y-N / NI-PC-DB
➤ (size of age difference — its effect now vs. later in life — best age to marry at first time around)

234. **BAGGAGE: Everyone enters a marriage with baggage.**
. ...T-F / NI-PC-DB
➤ (Should baggage be shared? — Does the age of the baggage matter? — Can sharing baggage make you appear more honest & trustworthy?)

235. **BORING: Can too much compatibility be boring?**.........
....Y-N / NI-PC-DB

236. **COMPROMISE: Success in marriage always involves compromise & sacrifice.**...........................T-F / NI-PC-DB
➤ (Is compromise a sign of weakness? — If a compromise is agreed upon happily & willingly without regret, pressure or resentment is it a compromise or a simple favor & act of kindness?)

237. **CONTRACT: Is marriage a contract?**..........Y-N / NI-PC-DB
➤ (What are the terms of a marriage beyond vows? — Does it require an element of surrender & the relinquishing of control? — How do you feel about prenups & wills, especially if children from previous marriages are involved?)

238. **COW MILK: Do you agree with the saying, "Why buy the cow when you can get the milk for free"?**
....Y-N / NI-PC-DB

239. **DIFFICULTY: The first two years of marriage are the hardest.**. ....T-F / NI-PC-DB

— Marriage —

240. **DIFFICULTY: Are marriages — A.** more difficult if the partners have separate career paths, **B.** more difficult if the partners are in business together, **C.** less difficult if one works & the other stays home, **D.** other ....
....**A-B-C-D / NI-PC-DB**
➤ If in separate careers & major conflicts arise around career obligations & time together, how would you decide whose life or whose career is most important?)

241. **DIVORCE: What are common reasons given for divorce or ending a relationship?** ....**NI-PC-DB**
➤ (money — cheating — a new love — incompatible goals — substance abuse — big & little lies & loss of trust — little or poor communications — children — in-laws — health issues — fell out of love — grew apart — aging — changes in appearance— neurosis of either or both parties — low self-esteem — lack of romance — sexual problems — physical disabilities — physical or emotional abuse — temper — low boiling point — irreconcilable differences — cross dressing — spiritual differences — change in gender identification — control issues — hygiene issues — too many annoying habits — judgmental, picky & petty — boredom — career conflicts — delusions & unrealistic, romanticized notions of what a relationship is all about — lack of commitment — distance — nothing in common — passionless — attitude or personality— How would you handle name changes after a divorce? — Are there better solutions to incompatibility issues other than divorce? — Would you stay in the house you lived in together, after the divorce?)

242. **DIVORCE: What is the most common reason why unhappy marriages do not end in divorce? — A.** financial issues, **B.** religious vows, **C.** children issues, **D.** the insecurity of one or both partners, **E.** protect appearances, **F.** too many obstacles to starting over, **G.** legal issues, **H.** other? ....**A-B-C-D-E-F G H / NI-PC-DB**

— Marriage —

243. **DIVORCE: The divorce rate is highest among celebrities.**...T-F / NI-PC-DB
➤ (If true, why?)

244. **ENGAGEMENT: When considering marriage, do you foresee — A. a short engagement, B. a long engagement, C. other?**...........................A-B-C / NI-PC-DB
➤ (Does a long engagement guarantee that any major incompatibilities will be revealed?)

245. **FAITH: Getting married requires a leap of faith.**.............
....T-F / NI-PC-DB

246. **FAMILY: How important is it to get to know the family of your life partner? — A. very, B. somewhat, C. not really**...A-B-C / NI-PC-DB
➤ (Is their approval of your relationship important to you? — Do they approve? — How do you feel about having your picture taken at family events? — If you married interracially or the same gender, how would your friends and family react?)

247. **FINANCIAL DECISIONS: Should the cost of large purchases require a joint decision?**........Y-N / NI-PC-DB
➤ (cars — major appliances — investments — charitable contributions — facelifts — vacations — honeymoon — jewelry — house — life insurance — hobbies — toys, **e.g.,** motorcycle — boat — big screen TV — etc.)

248. **FRIEND: Your spouse should be your best friend.**.........
....T-F / NI-PC-DB

249. **FULFILLING: What distinguishes a good marriage from a fulfilling one?**...NI-PC-DB

250. **FUN: Being married can be more fun than dating.**.........
....T-F / NI-PC-DB

— Marriage —

251. **HAPPINESS: If you're unhappy, getting married can make you happy.**..T-F / NI-PC-DB
➤ (Who's responsible for your happiness?)

252. **HAPPINESS: Being in a committed relationship is necessary to be truly happy.** ....T-F / NI-PC-DB

253. **HEALTH: Do you agree with studies that contend that happily married people are healthier than unmarried or unhappily married people?** ....Y-N / NI-PC-DB

254. **INTELLIGENCE: Intellectual compatibility in a relationship is a major indicator of long-term success & happiness in marriage.** ....T-F / NI-PC-DB
➤ (academic interests — variance in SAT scores — IQ — interest in mind development — common sense — street smarts — wit)

255. **LAST NAME: Which last name do you prefer after getting married? — A. maiden, B. husband's, C. combination, D. separate** ....A-B-C-D / NI-PC-DB
➤ (Is not wearing a wedding ring off-the-table?)

256. **MINOR CHILDREN: How important is your partner's relationship with your minor children? — A. very, B. moderately, C. somewhat, D. not at all** ....
....A-B-C-D / NI-PC-DB

257. **MOTIVATION: Is being madly in love sufficient reason to get married?** ....Y-N / NI-PC-DB
➤ (Is marriage on or off the table?)

— Marriage —

258. **PARTNER: Would any of the following individuals be excluded as a potential marriage partner?**
....Y-N / NI-PC-DB
➤ (someone previously married — currently in the military — a non-citizen — a criminal — a cop — not of same race — not of same religion — has children — doesn't like or want children — someone poor — someone who lacks ambition — someone unexcited about their future — someone who wanted to live where you don't — too old — too young — not attractive enough — other)

259. **PERMISSION: Is getting permission to marry from the father &/or mother of your partner a good idea?**.........
....Y-N / NI-PC-DB

260. **PERSONALITY: A relationship between a dominant & a passive partner has a better chance of success than two dominants.**....................................T-F / NI-PC-DB

261. **PERSONALITY: The 'right' person will put up with your flaws, faults & shortcomings & not try to change you.** ....T-F / NI-PC-DB
➤ (Do you unconditionally accept yourself with all your flaws?)

262. **PREVIOUS: Do subsequent marriages benefit from lessons learned in previous marriages?** ....
....Y-N / NI-PC-DB
➤ (Does hope spring eternal? — Is the grass always greener? — Is the divorce rate higher or lower among those once divorced?)

263. **PROBLEMS: As a married couple, there is no 'your' problem or 'their' problem, every problem is an 'our' problem.** ....T-F / NI-PC-DB
➤ (Does the same apply to money?)

264. **QUALITY: A good marriage depends on having common interests & compatible goals.** (see **Common Interests** under **Relationships** main heading) ....T-F / NI-PC-DB

— Marriage —

265. **RESULT: In a marriage, two people become one.**...........
....T-F / NI-PC-DB

266. **STATUS: Are you married — engaged — separated — widowed — divorced — single?** ....NI-PC-DB
➤ (number of times married or engaged — single but want to be married — married but want to be single)

267. **TOLERANCE: Could a partner's idiosyncrasies or quirks make a marriage untenable?** ....Y-N / NI-PC-DB

268. **TYPE: What kind of a wedding did you have or want?** .
....NI-PC-DB
➤ (civil — religious — What kind of marriages are there, **e.g.,** open — common-law — shotgun — sham — arranged — bigamous — polygamous — green card — marriage of convenience? — Polyamorous — Who pays for the wedding?)

269. **VOWS: What does the vow 'to love honor & cherish, for better or worse, till death do us part' mean?** ....
....NI-PC-DB
➤ (If one partner defaults on the vow, does that free the other partner to ignore the vow?)

270. **WEDDING: When considering marriage, do you foresee — A. a large formal wedding, B. a small, quiet, intimate affair, C. eloping, D. a simple courthouse ceremony, E. a destination wedding?** .A-B-C-D E / NI-PC-DB
➤ (Who will pay for the wedding?)

— Marriage —

271. WHY: Why do people get married? ....NI-PC-DB
➤ (love — companionship — friendship — co-pilot — life-partner — financial, **i.e.,** money — a meal ticket — legal benefits — or security — physical attraction — great personality — emotional security — caregiver — house-keeper — handyman — nurse with a purse — playmate — trophy-mate — status — bound by a similar loss or tragedy — looking for a, **i.e.,** rescuer — defender — protector — a sounding board — a brainstorming partner — a confidant — or a mirror — sex — pregnancy — children & grandchildren — convenience — please others, **i.e.,** parents — grandparents — or adult children — public appearances — to get out of the house — to insure inheritance — insurance benefits — family rights — power of attorney — partners in crime — to be part of a prestigious family name — green card — bored with dating — greater sense of meaning & purpose — guaranteed date on Friday & Saturday nights — demonstration of commitment — increase in trustworthiness — other — Is marriage just a piece of paper?)

272. WORDS: How would hearing the words, "I want to spend the rest of my life with you" affect you? ....
....NI-PC-DB

273. WORK: Does marriage — A. take work, B. it shouldn't take work ....A-B / NI-PC-DB

See also Dating, Live-in, Love, Sex, Relationships, Communications main headings.

14. **MISCELLANEOUS**

Important! Please read.

TABLE OF CONTENTS — Page 5

23 Chapters Listed Alphabetically — 723 Main Questions —

Key words in each chapter are in alphabetical order for that chapter.

ANSWER CHOICES

Y-N (Yes No) — T-F (True False) — A-B-C (Multiple Choice)

NI (Non-Issue) — PC (Potential Conflict) — DB (Deal Breaker)

HOW TO ADDRESS THE QUESTIONS

Whether you're in a relationship or not, answer first for yourself, then ask yourself, how would you feel if your partner or a potential partner were to choose differently or the opposite? If reviewing with a partner and areas of disagreement arise, engage your sense of humor, remain calm, and discuss your differences civilly.

JUDGING AN ENTRY

Whatever you feel about an entry, be careful not to underestimate the value of what may appear to be a petty or trivial issue. You'd be surprised, or maybe not, at how little it can take to start an argument or reveal a difference of opinion. A discussion of these minor issues can sometimes be quite revelatory.

RIGHT & WRONG

Keep in mind there are no absolutely right or wrong answers, just your subjective opinions expressed as a starting point for deliberation or discussion.

☆☆☆☆☆

— Miscellaneous —

274. **ACTIVIST: Are you an activist or advocate for a cause you're committed to that demands much of your time & attention?** ....**Y-N / NI-PC-DB**
➤ (How would you respond to a love interest who complained that your involvement was taking away too much of your time & attention from them?)

275. **ADDICTIONS: We are all addicted to or obsessed with something.** ....**T-F / NI-PC-DB**
➤ (e.g., our convictions — power — hobbies — money — fame — pleasure seeking — cell phone — texting — gaming — politics — news — soaps — celebrities — our loves —fears — hates — lies — food — drugs — alcohol — gambling — sex — the past — Do you believe sexual addiction is a disease that can ruin marriages & tear families apart? — Is it fair to consider an addiction as any habit that can't be given up without anxiety, or other withdrawal symptoms? — Is anyone addiction-free?)

276. **APPETITES: Legislation aimed at changing human appetites re: sex, sugar, cigarettes, drugs, alcohol, etc., has little effect on changing the psychology of human behavior, even if the behavior is immoral, self-defeating, or expensive.** ....**T-F / NI-PC-DB**

277. **AREAS OF LIFE: If you could live your life over again, which area or areas of life would you change? — A. romantic relationship choices, B. career or job choices, C. religious or spiritual foundation, D. attitudes toward family, E. educational choices, F. eating habits, G. exercise habits, H. alcohol, drinking or drug habits** ....
....**A-B-C-D-E-F G / NI-PC-DB**

— Miscellaneous —

278. **AUTOMOBILE: What are your preferences when acquiring an automobile?**..............................**NI-PC-DB**
➤ (buy or lease — new or used — luxury — economy — practical — high performance — sport — classic — kit — SUV — truck van — convertible or hardtop — compact — midsize — full-size — clean electric — hybrid — hydrogen — self-driving — cost — Is your choice affected by gas prices? — What's your car's timeline history — How many vehicles do you own?)

279. **BEAUTY CONTESTS: What's your attitude toward beauty contests for children vs. for adults?**...**NI-PC-DB**

280. **BODY CHEMISTRY: Can body chemistry be changed by our thoughts?** ....**Y-N / NI-PC-DB**
➤ (fear — hate — anger — resentment — anxiety — depression — love — joy — excitement — envy — jealousy)

281. **BULLYING: When being bullied, which is the preferred response — A. turn the other cheek, B. react in kind, C. react with twice the force, D. respond with wit, E. walk away, F. call for help** ....**A-B-C D-E-F / NI-PC-DB**

282. **CAKE: What does the phrase 'have your cake & eat it, too' mean?** ....**NI-PC-DB**

283. **CANNIBALISM: Would you resort to cannibalism if necessary to survive in a life & death situation?**.........
....**Y-N / NI-PC-DB**

284. **CATASTROPHES: Which of the following do you consider most terrifying? — A. an earthquake, B. a hurricane-cyclone-typhoon, C. a tornado, D. a tsunami, E. a fire, F. mud slides, G. a pandemic virus**
....**A-B-C-D-E-F G / NI-PC-DB**

— Miscellaneous —

285. **CELEBRITIES: Are you obsessed with or fanatical about celebrities?** ....**Y-N / NI-PC-DB**
➤ (Keeping Up With the Kardashians — Celebrity Big Brother — Celebrity Apprentice — Have you ever been a screaming fan of anyone?)

286. **CLIMATE CHANGE: Climate change is — A.** mostly man-made, **B.** mostly the result of natural climate cycles, **C.** some combination, **D.** a hoax, **E.** much more complicated than most laymen understand ....
....**A-B-C-D-E / NI-PC-DB**

287. **CLONING: What is your attitude toward cloning?**
....**NI-PC-DB**
➤ (mammals — primates — monkeys — polo horses)

288. **COMMUNITY: Are you involved in your community?** ....
....**Y-N / NI-PC-DB**
➤ (service — charity — civic duty — voting — meetings — social events — politics)

289. **COMPLIMENTS: How often do you receive positive feedback? — A.** daily, **B.** weekly, **C.** monthly, **D.** rarely ...
....**A-B-C-D / NI-PC-DB**
➤ (compliments, **e.g.,** good job — nice work — psychological strokes — hugs — expressions of love — pats on the back — applause — a thank you — bonuses — raises — awards — plaques — certificates of appreciation — gifts — a special parking place — a paid day-off — special recognition — testimonials or positive reviews — etc. — What's the difference between wanting recognition & wanting attention?)

— Miscellaneous —

290. **CONSPIRACIES: Do you embrace conspiracy theories surrounding any of the following?**...........Y-N / NI-PC-DB
➤ (2020 election winner — 9-11 — the weather — JFK assassination — the moon landing — Area 51 — Sandy Hook & Parkland Elementary — Elvis — Coronavirus-19 — QAnon — Jeffry Epstein's death — Osama Bin Laden wasn't killed — etc. — Do you believe we've been visited by extraterrestrials?)

291. **CUSSING: Does swearing & bad language bother you?** ....Y-N / NI-PC-DB
➤ (Do you consider yourself prudish?)

292. **DEATH: Are you prepared physically, emotionally & psychologically for death or dying re: yourself or a loved one?** ....NI-PC-DB
➤ (cemetery plot — funeral — cryogenics — physician assisted suicide — cremation — burial — euthanasia — living will — mourning — handling a terminal illness — hospice — memorial — public announcements — eulogy —Are you concerned with dying or the prospect of dying in pain? — Are you concerned with dying slowly over a period of time & being a burden to others? — Are you concerned with the afterlife? — Would you continue to live in the home where your spouse died?)

293. **DECISIONS: When making decisions, for which are you likely to pay the greater price for being wrong?**
— **A.** being overly optimistic, **B.** overly pessimistic...........
....A-B / NI-PC-DB
➤ (Which decisions, if wrong, are likely to be the most costly, those involving finances or those involving relationships? — Were your major life decisions dictated more by money or passion?)

294. **DECISIONS: Have the proverbs, "The early bird gets the worm but the second mouse gets the cheese" ever helped you make a decision?**...........Y-N / NI-PC-DB

— Miscellaneous —

295. **DECISIONS: In an issue involving a close call between 'law & order' vs. personal freedom, civil liberties, or privacy rights, which would you side with?** — **A.** law & order, **B.** personal freedom, **C.** civil liberties, **D.** privacy rights...**A-B-C-D / NI-PC-DB**

296. **DECISIONS: Is it human nature to attempt to defend, deny, justify & rationalize one's mistakes, poor decisions & bad actions?**...........................**Y-N / NI-PC-DB**
➤ (Have you made dumb decisions? — Are many of your bad decisions dumb or simply explained with the phrase 'unintended or unforeseen consequences'? — How comfortable are you saying, "I was wrong, I made a dumb mistake, forgive me, it was my fault, I'm truly sorry?" — How often do you hear it? — How do you feel about the philosophy, 'act now without permission, apologize & ask for forgiveness later'? — How many major decisions have you made in your lifetime that, if you knew then what you know now, you would have chosen differently? — Have you ever faced a 'Sophie's Choice,' an impossible no-win set of options, similar to ethical dilemmas & the 'all-or-none' Hobson's Choice?)

297. **DESTINY & FATE: Do you believe in destiny or fate?** ....
....**Y-N / NI-PC-DB**
➤ (events & the future are predetermined at birth— things are meant to be — events are, **e.g.,** preordained — inevitable — imminent — impending — or doomed — choice has little influence — opposite of free will — little personal responsibility)

298. **DISCUSSIONS: Discussions of politics or religion should be avoided in social situations, among certain friends & family members, or at work.** ....
....**T-F / NI-PC-DB**

299. **DEVIL: Have you ever made a decision based on the phrase, 'Better the devil you know, than the devil you don't know'?** ....**Y-N / NI-PC-DB**
➤ (Does this idea sometimes prevent people from ending unsatisfying relationships?)

— Miscellaneous —

300. **DISGUSTS & HATES: Do you have any disgusts hates, or intense dislikes? — A. many, B. a few, C. none?** ......
....A-B-C / NI-PC-DB
➤ (What are they? — Were they acquired in childhood or as an adult?)

301. **DREAMS: What is the state of your dreams?** ....NI-PC-DB
➤ (active in process — realistic & ambitious — fanciful, delusional & unrealistic — goals & plans are on paper — you're working on acquiring requisite skills — you're seeking necessary financing — you're hiring a support team — they reflect your hidden talents yearning to be expressed)

302. **DREAMS: Do you have dreams so motivating that they wake you up in the morning excited about life?**
....Y-N / NI-PC-DB
➤ (Are your dreams so exciting that even your disappointments are viewed as nothing more than challenging learning experiences?)

303. **DREAMS: Never give up on your dreams.** ....
....T-F / NI-PC-DB
➤ (If false, when & under what circumstances should dreams be forsaken? — How will you decide if you're hanging on too long or giving up to soon?)

304. **DRIVING HABITS: Do you consider yourself to be a good driver?** ....Y-N / NI-PC-DB
➤ (Do you engage in road rage or excessive speed? — Do you often ignore traffic rules & signals? — Do you consider yourself accident prone? — Has your auto insurance been affected by your driving record? — Do you text or use your cell phone while driving? — If you've had accidents, what do you blame them on?)

— Miscellaneous —

305. **EMAIL: Are you overwhelmed with email?**......................
....**Y-N / NI-PC-DB**

➤ (Do you get more email than you can handle? — Do you organize your email? — Is most of it useless? — Is some of it very important? — Do you prefer to call, write, text, or email? — How often do you read your email? — How often to you clean up your mailbox?)

306. **ETHICAL DILEMMAS: When confronted with an ethical dilemma, do you respond by — A. doing the right thing (who defines 'right'), B. doing the unselfish thing, C. doing the thing that's hard to do, D. doing what's necessary even if against your own self-interest, E. all of the above, F. doing nothing?** ....**A-B-C-D-E-F / NI-PC-DB**

➤ (Would you hesitate to be a whistle blower involving corruption in an institution, **i.e.,** corporate, police, military, medical, political, governmental — etc.? — What would you do if you witnessed grossly inappropriate behavior in a public place or business establishment involving harassment, cheating or stealing from a tip jar — harassment of a waitress by a customer — extreme prejudicial judgment of a class of people — mistreatment of a child or pet — mugging on a subway platform? — situational ethics — Can you remember any specific moral, financial, educational, career, or love dilemmas you may have ever had?)

307. **FAVORS: What is your attitude toward being asked for favors?** ....**NI-PC-DB**

➤ Does it depend on who's asking, **e.g.,** a friend — a friend on behalf of a friend — an acquaintance — a work associate — a family member? — Does it depend on whether or not you make a living with the skill being requested? — Does it depend on how long the favor is estimated to take? — Have you had many experiences where your good nature has been taken advantage of? — Is it called 'quid-pro-quo' if you expect the favor will someday be returned? — Do you believe in the idea of 'pay-it-forward'?)

— Miscellaneous —

308. **FEARS: What are you afraid of, very concerned about, or the thought of it scares you?** ....**NI-PC-DB**

➤ (poverty — bankruptcy — no health care — debilitating illness or disease — total disability — old age — being a burden — being sued or labeled as a sex offender — being used for your money — career failure — cancel culture — loss of a loved one — betrayal by a loved one — being rejected by a loved one — being embarrassed by a partner — not being loved — being body-shamed — being totally alone — being assaulted, raped, or robbed — vaccines — side effects of drugs — hearing a break-in at night while in bed — public humiliation — gossip — airplanes take-offs & landings — roller coasters — being blackmailed — being ridiculed or stigmatized — cyber-bullying — boredom — commitment — being swallowed up by a sinkhole – public speaking — ostracism — being judged unjustly of a crime or offense you didn't commit — loss of sight, taste, hearing, or a limb — death **re:** dying in disgrace — buried alive — drowning — freezing or burning to death — dying by any means — spiders — civil war — losing your cell phone — porch pirates — extremists **re:** political, religious, or environmental — identify theft — extreme weather — global warming — natural disasters — a plague or a pandemic virus — fires — floods — power outages — cyber attacks on water treatment plants — cloning — terrorism — insurrection — being a victim of a mass shooting — nuclear war — water or air pollution — food poisoning due to tainted or contaminated food — internet surveillance — invasion of privacy — government & political corruption — clowns — waking up nude in front of an audience — retaliation by an enemy or someone you've hurt — losing your job to technology or someone younger — being hacked — losing all of your computer or phone data — revenge porn — demise of our democracy — Do you often buy extended warrantees? — Have any of your fears caused you nightmares? — How long do you think you could handle prison or solitary confinement, with reason to hope vs. without hope of ever being free again? — How well did you or are you handling Covid ? — How far would you go in responding to lies told about you & your character? — Are you obsessed with the need for high-tech home security? — After experiencing a scary or life-threatening event, do you focus on what could have happened, what didn't happen, or how to avoid such an event in the future?)

— Miscellaneous —

309. **FUNERALS & MEMORIALS: What's your attitude toward attending funerals & memorials?**........NI-PC-DB

➤ (Does your attitude depend on whether the deceased is a family member — a friend — a work associate — a celebrity — a famous person — a humanitarian — or a loved one — What kind of funeral do you visualize for yourself **re:** size, guests, location, cost?

310. **GARDENING: Do you have — A. a green thumb, B. a brown thumb?** ....A-B / NI-PC-DB

311. **GASLIGHTING: Have you ever experienced or been a target of gaslighting?** ....Y-N / NI-PC-DB

➤ (It's defined as a form of psychological manipulation, or crazy-making, that seeks to sow seeds of doubt in a targeted individual or members of a group. — It's intent is to destabilize the target & delegitimize their belief(s). — It's based on making them question their own memory, perception & sanity. — It employs persistent denial, misdirection, contradiction & lies.)

312. **GHOSTS: What percent of the population do you think believes in ghosts? — A. 10% or under, B. 11 to 25%, C. 26 to 50%, D. over 50%?** ....A-B-C-D / NI-PC-DB

➤ (How does belief in them affect the believer's behavior?) — (Do you believe in them?)

313. **GIFTS: What's your attitude toward giving & getting gifts?** ....NI-PC-DB

➤ (to & from whom — purpose of gift — cost — exchanging gifts — returning gifts — disappointing gifts — expectations — holidays — birthdays — anniversaries — regifting — gift-cards)

314. **GUILT: Do you have — A. a lot of guilt, B. some, C. a little?** ....A-B-C / NI-PC-DB

➤ (Are you susceptible to being guilt-tripped? — Does your guilt include regret? — Does asking for forgiveness & being forgiven reduce feelings of guilt?)

— Miscellaneous —

315. **HELL: "The road to hell is paved with good intentions."** ....T-F / NI-PC-DB
➤ (Have you ever suffered negative consequences as a result of your good intentions?)

316. **HITCHHIKERS: How do you feel about picking up hitchhikers.— <u>A. very willing, B. have done so, C. never would?</u>** ....A-B-C / NI-PC-DB
➤ (Does your answer depend on, **e.g.,** the gender, appearance or age of the hitchhiker — the location — time of day — your mood — other?)

317. **HOLIDAYS: How do you typically celebrate these holidays & special days?** ....NI-PC-DB
➤ (New Year's Eve & day — Valentines Day — Independence Day — Halloween — Thanksgiving — Christmas — Mother's Day — Father's Day)

318. **HUNTING: Does hunting help animal conservation?** .....
....Y-N / NI-PC-DB
➤ (What effect does it have on control of, **e.g.,** predators.— habitats — vegetation — population — biodiversity — diseases — ecosystems — food — community development — etc.? — How do you feel about trophy hunting, **e.g.,** rhino horns — elephant tusks — antlers — heads — skins — or furs?)

319. **HYPNOSIS: Can a legitimately hypnotized subject be talked into doing something against their conscience or will, such as having sex with someone underage, or killing someone?** ....
....Y-N / NI-PC-DB
➤ (If yes, can such acts legally be considered rape & murder? — Which is a stronger motivator: the impulse to do the right thing, or the guilt for not doing it?) — Can genetics be a defense for murder? — Is hypnosis magic or simply heightened suggestibility?)

— Miscellaneous —

320. **HYPOCRISY: Is being hypocritical — A.** a normal, inherent, human shortcoming, **B.** a sign of the times, **C.** an unadmirable trait? ....**A-B C / NI-PC-DB**
➤ (Is anyone free of hypocrisy? — Do you live by all of what you preach or teach?)

321. **INFLUENCE: Who has the greater influence on your life — A.** your God, **B.** the Pope, **C.** the President, **D.** your parents, **E.** your partner, **F.** your BFF, **G.** your therapist, **H.** local politicians, **I.** local judges, **J.** your 'tribe-gang-crew-club', **K.** you, your intelligence & common sense ....**A-B-C-D-E-F-G-H-I-J K / NI-PC-DB**
➤ (Whose opinions most strongly influence your decision making? — Who are your decision-making, brainstorming partners? — What percent of your life turned out as planned? — Who is most responsible for why life isn't working, as well as planned or expected?)

322. **JURY DUTY: On a jury, if asked, would you accept the position of jury foreperson?** ....**Y-N / NI-PC-DB**
➤ (Can you imagine being the lone holdout on a jury, whether to convict or acquit? — Have you ever served on a jury? — Have you ever exercised a way to avoid jury duty?)

323. **JUSTICE: Do you believe justice in our legal system is — A.** blind & fair, **B.** favors the rich, **C.** disfavors the poor, **D.** is better than the alternatives...**A-B-C-D / NI-PC-DB**
➤ (What are the alternatives to our system of justice? — more & stricter laws — more emphasis on rehabilitation — less emphasis on punishment — How effective is ostracism & the cancel culture?)

324. **LEGAL: Do you have any civil or criminal issues pending?** ....**Y-N / NI-PC-DB**
➤ (problems with IRS — divorce proceedings — DUI — custody issues — business or personal lawsuits — landlord tenant issues — patent or copyright problems — other)

— Miscellaneous —

325. **LENDING: What your attitude toward lending?** ....
....NI-PC-DB
➤ (money — books — clothes — tools — technology equipment —
Would you lend your car to, **e.g.,** a friend — family member —
business associate — or a boy-or girlfriend? — How do you
respond when you don't get back what you've lent?)

326. **LIFE: Has life become more complicated, more
difficult & more troublesome than you previously
thought it would be?** ....Y-N / NI-PC-DB
➤ (On a scale of 1 to 10, how perfect is your life?)

327. **LIFE: Are you satisfied with the life you've led up until
now?** ....Y-N / NI-PC-DB
➤ (your legacy — your accomplishments — How happy you are?
e.g., ecstatically & gloriously happy — very happy — happy
enough — not so happy — unhappy — very unhappy — need help?
— Would you be okay if you were to die tomorrow? — Do you need
more time to make your mark or fulfill your calling? — What steps
did you take today to improve the quality of your life in all 8-areas —
mental — physical — emotional —spiritual — social — financial —
family — career? — Have you planned for the future? — Are you
living your plan? — What is your current biggest obstacle to making
progress toward achieving your goals & dreams?)

328. **LUXURIOUS ACCESSORIES: Do you desire luxurious
accessories?** ....Y-N / NI-PC-DB
➤ (Are you inclined to flaunt them? — Are you envious of people
who have them? — Can you afford them?)

329. **MAGIC: Do you like magic &/or card tricks?** ....
....Y-N / NI-PC-DB

330. **MARK: Everyone wants to make their mark or make a
difference.** ....T-F / NI-PC-DB

331. **MARS: Should we invest in going to Mars &/or back to
the moon?** ....Y-N / NI-PC-DB

— Miscellaneous —

332. **MEMORY: In your opinion, is your memory** — **A.** good, **B.** bad, **C.** average? ....**A-B-C / NI-PC-DB**
➤ (Do others question your memory? — Are you aware of cell & muscle memory? — Can you consciously erase 'bad' or intrusive memories? — Do you know the difference between repressed & suppressed memories? — What do you know about recovered & false memories? — How important to your present mental & emotional health are your memories of the past? — Which of your memories are most memorable, the very pleasurable or the most painful?)

333. **MEMORY: Which do you hold most responsible for your 'bad' memory?** — **A.** your defective brain, **B.** unapplied memory techniques, **C.** nutrition, **D.** sleep habits, **E.** worry & preoccupations, **F.** age or age related diseases, **G.** a self-fulfilling prophecy, **H.** other ....
....**A-B-C-D-E-F-G-H / NI-PC-DB**
➤ (Do you take supplements to improve your memory? — How have you come to the conclusion that you have a particularly bad memory, by what standard, compared to what, compared to whom?)

— Miscellaneous —

334. MORALITY: What's your attitude toward lying & cheating? ....NI-PC-DB

➤ (cheating on taxes by not declaring cash-income or exaggerating expenses — cheating at cards or board games — stealing — have you ever stolen anything — breaking the 10 commandments — jumping theaters to see two movies on one admission — **lying about:** your age or that of your kids to get price breaks — about having an orgasm — about having a headache to avoid sex — **lying to:** your boss to get time off — to debt collectors — to portray yourself in a more positive light — to cover up something you're not proud of — to impress the opposite sex — to protect another's feelings, sweet lies — to get off the phone using fake static — **lying on:** employment, loan, or admissions applications — your Facebook profile — If someone lies about little things, can they be trusted to tell the truth about big issues? — Would ever again trust someone whom you knew snooped a look in you bathroom medicine cabinet? — Which is worse, a liar, a hypocrite, or a thief? — Are you familiar with the concept of 'false moral equivalency'? — Are all lies equal or do they fall on a continuum of significance from white lies to deal breakers? — How important is the purpose or reason for lying when measuring the materiality of the lie? — Is it okay to lie when the truth is not helpful? — Have you ever been called truthful or honest to a fault? — Is there anything more damaging to a relationship than lying to & cheating on one's mate? — Is it a lie if the alleged liar believes they were telling the truth? — Would you share with a friend the knowledge that their partner was having an affair? — Are your morality standards rigid or flexible depending on context **re:** who, what, why, where, when & how? — Is there a price for lying even if you don't get caught? — Have you heard of cognitive dissonance related to guilt? — What does an unprovoked denial suggest? — Do animals lie? — Would you lie to your partner about drinking or smoking behind their back? — If you received a gift you hated, would you say to the donor, you loved it?)

— Miscellaneous —

335. **MOTIVATION: Which of the following wants, needs & desires currently reflect your motivation?** .....NI-PC-DB
➤ What are you passionate about? — Which words are moving you to action? — preoccupations, **e.g.,** money — sex — love — ambition — power — control — appreciation — forgiveness — acceptance for who you are — a promotion — adulation — more leisure time — more freedom — improved health — surgery — start a family — to feel good about yourself — to be recognized for your accomplishments —to be popular — to complete projects in process — to leave a legacy — to express your creativity — to travel — to be of service — to live adventurously — to expand your knowledge — to have peace of mind — hobbies — social time — to be the best at something — to be a good role model — to make a difference — to make your mark — to change the world — to prepare for an afterlife — to find meaning & purpose — other?)

336. **MOTIVATION: What's the most exciting thing currently going on in your life?** ....NI-PC-DB
➤ (Does it involve arts & entertainment — money — closing a big sale or business deal — getting an award or recognition — a relationship — creativity — a challenge — a new purchase — children — a vacation — travel — a major project — other?)

337. **MOURNING: What variables explain why everyone grieves in their own way?** ....NI-PC-DB
➤ (What does it mean when we say some people deal with death & grief better than others? — Have you ever questioned or doubted the legitimacy of another's love for the deceased by how they demonstrated their grief over their loss?)

— Miscellaneous —

338. **MULTI-TASKING: Multi-tasking is** — **A.** a time-saver **B.** hardly possible, **C.**possible only if the tasks don't require focus or creative thought, **D.** often self-defeating ....
....**A-B C-D / NI-PC-DB**
➤ (Which of the following is or is not an effective way to multi-task? — reading on the toilet — doing the dishes while watching TV — editing a book while on the phone — doing your taxes while sorting your laundry — putting on makeup or shaving while driving your car — planning tomorrow while watching T.V — practicing a speech while doing your walk — reading during commercial breaks)

339. **NEWS: When reading or listening to the news, do you generally prefer**— **A.** headlines, **B.** full back stories & details? ....**A-B / NI-PC-DB**
➤ (When hearing about someone's day, do you prefer highlights or specifics? — Generally speaking, do you prefer summaries, condensations, digest versions, or detailed explanations & expanded versions? — Do you bury the lead when telling stories or begin with it? — Do you prefer short stories or novels? — Is 'time' & being too busy the issue that governs your answers?)

340. **NEWS: Is most news** — **A.** fake, partisan & full of lies, **B.** fair, basically accurate, worth your attention, **C.** journalistically responsible? ....**A-B-C / NI-PC-DB**
➤ (Does your answer depend on the source? — Are you familiar with 'catch & kill' re: news articles? — Do you distrust selected news networks? — Do you agree that fake news travels six times faster, farther, broader & deeper than the truth? — Have you heard the quote, "A lie can travel half way around the world while the truth is putting on its shoes.")

341. **NEWS: When waiting on or expecting feedback from a business associate, sales prospect, friend, mechanic, or doctor, do you typically consider 'no news' as**— **A.** good news, **B.** bad news? ...**A-B / NI-PC-DB**

— Miscellaneous —

342. **NEW YEAR'S RESOLUTIONS: Do you — A.** make &
keep New Year's resolutions, **B.** make & not keep them,
C. don't make them? ....**A-B-C / NI-PC-DB**
➤ (Have you made any of these common resolutions, **e.g.,** be a
better person — lose weight — exercise more — eat healthier —
get a better job — improve overall health — quit smoking — spend
less — other?)

343. **PARANORMAL-METAPHYSICAL-SUPERNATURAL:**
Which of the following do you believe in? ....
....**Y-N / NI-PC-DB**
➤ (astrology — numerology — tarot cards — seances — past lives
— witchcraft — psychics — ESP — fortune tellers — fortune
cookies — mediums — spirits — ghosts — voodoo — curses —
chakras — clairvoyance — 6th sense — telekinesis — telepathy —
precognition — prescience — mysticism — sorcery — tea leaves —
Ouija boards — alchemy — ESP — Do you have psychic abilities?
— Big Foot — Loch Ness Monster — alien visitors — things that are
inexplicable — Do you believe there are mysteries in the world that
can't be explained by science? — How does knowing something
differ from believing something, or having faith that something is
true? — Which do you trust more: science, intuition, common
sense, conspiracy theories, political leaders, the press, other? — do
you believe in magic?)

344. **PEEING: Is peeing in the shower — A.** okay, **B.** not
okay? ....**A-B / NI-PC-DB**

345. **PETA: Are you — A.** pro PETA, an animal advocacy
activist, **B.** anti-PETA? ....**A-B / NI-PC-DB**
➤ (What's your attitude toward caged animals for entertainment or
education in zoos, circuses & aquariums? — How do you feel about
caged animals in factory farming, **e.g.,** pigs in crates — hens &
dairy cows in confined spaces — etc.? — How do you feel about
hunting for food — trophy hunting — hunting for environmental
conservation — steps to protect the extinction of of a species, **e.g.,**
elephants — killer whales — dolphins — lions — tigers — primates
— etc.?)

— Miscellaneous —

346. **PETS: What's your attitude toward pets?** ....NI-PC-DB
➤ (Are you a dog or cat person? — Do you own pets? — Do you want or not want them?— allergies — time & cost to care for them — size preference — Would you treat it as a family member? — Is there any limit to how much you would spend on extraordinary life-saving efforts? —How do you feel about, **e.g.,** Pit Bulls & their reputation — service dogs — on the toilet training for cats — declawing cats — other pets, **e.g.,** horses — snakes — birds — pot-bellied pigs — hamsters — exotic animals — a cloned horse? — What's your favorite animal? — Would you kiss your dog on the mouth or let it lick your face? — Would you let your dog or pet sleep in bed with you?)

347. **PIERCINGS: Do you have any piercings?** ....
....Y-N / NI-PC-DB
➤ (how many — size — location — cost — Have they been problematic?)

348. **PLANTS: Plants are sentient, feel pain & respond to being talked to.** ....T-F / NI-PC-DB

349. **PLANTS: Are you a plant person?** ....Y-N / NI-PC-DB
➤ (indoor or outdoor — potted or grounded — small or large — flowers — maintenance demands — rare or common)

350. **POLITICAL CORRECTNESS: What are the effects of political correctness?** — **A.** stifles humor & open, honest, spontaneous communication, **B.** reduces the likelihood of offending, insulting, or marginalizing certain groups, **C.** raises awareness of social discrimination & injustice, **D.** all the above ....A-B-C-D / NI-PC-DB

— *Miscellaneous* —

351. **PREOCCUPATION: In relation to the hierarchy of needs, which is your current highest priority & greatest preoccupation? — A.** physical & biological, **B.** safety & security, **C.** social & love, **D.** ego & esteem, **E.** self-fulfillment & self-actualization ......**A-B-C-D-E / NI-PC-DB**
➤ (Is your preoccupation, worry & anxiety externally imposed or self-imposed? — When you're preoccupied, is it more likely to be about what you want to happen, but fear it may not, or about what you don't want to happen, but fear it may?)

352. **PRIVACY: How important is your need for privacy & personal space? — A.** very, **B.** moderately, **C.** somewhat ....**A-B-C / NI-PC-DB**
➤ (How would you respond to the statement 'I need my space or more space'?)

353. **PROBLEMS: How often do you say, "if it's not one thing it's another"? — A.** too often, **B.** fairly often, **C.** occasionally, **D.** rarely ....**A-B-C-D / NI-PC-DB**
➤ (Do you address small problems & minor to-dos when they arise or only when they demand your attention?)

354. **PROTESTING: Do you find protests, e.g., kneeling by athletes during the national anthem at sporting events, or by movie stars at entertainment award events — A.** acceptable, **B.** unacceptable? ....
....**A-B / NI-PC-DB**

355. **PUBLICITY: There's no such thing as bad publicity.**.......
....**T-F / NI-PC-DB**
➤ (Is this the same as 'any publicity is good publicity'?)

356. **PUZZLES & RIDDLES: Do you — A.** like puzzles, riddles & tricks, **B.** don't like them? ....**A-B / NI-PC-DB**
➤ (Do you ever play Sudoku, crossword or jigsaw puzzles? — Do you like mysteries?)

— Miscellaneous —

357. **REGRETS: Do you have** — **A. many regrets, B. few, C none?** ....A-B-C / NI-PC-DB
➤ (Do you have more regrets for what you said or did or more for what you didn't say or didn't do?)

358. **RESTROOMS: How do you feel about using public restrooms?**...NI-PC-DB

359. **SCHADENFREUDE: What is your attitude toward people who take pleasure in learning of or witnessing the troubles, failures, or humiliation of others?** .... NI-PC-DB
➤ (Does your answer depend on whether the 'other' is a business competitor, an adversary, a politician of an opposing party, or a onetime friend who turned on you? — Is this the same as liking to see people get their comeuppance?)

360. **SEASONS: Which is your favorite season?** — **A. summer, B. fall, C. winter, D. spring** ......A-B-C-D / NI-PC-DB

361. **STATION-POSITION IN LIFE: In only a few words, where are you in your life?** ....NI-PC-DB
➤ (age — career — education — children — financial — relationship)

362. **SUICIDE: Are you** — **A. not okay with physician assisted suicide, B. okay with it?** ....A-B / NI-PC-DB

363. **SUPER POWERS: Which super power would you most prefer?** — **A. super strength, B. super hearing, C. x-ray vision, D. walk through walls, E. mind reading, F. the voice of an angel, G. taste of a super chef, H. fly like a bird, I. memory** ....A-B-C-D-E-F-G-H-I / NI-PC-DB

364. **TATOOS: Do you have any tattoos?** ....Y-N / NI-PC-DB
➤ (location — size — number — names of exes — written messages — Do they preclude getting an MRI? — Are there any you would like removed?)

— Miscellaneous —

365. **TEACHING: Do you believe we all teach by example, by what we do & how we live?** ....T-F / NI-PC-DB
➤ (What do you do that you don't want others to do? — What kind of a role-model are you?)

366. **TEASING: What's your attitude toward teasing or being teased?** ....NI-PC-DB
➤ (about, **e.g.,** your weight — fashion sense — smarts — looks — character — perspective & way of thinking — Do you consider yourself defensive, sensitive, thin-skinned, or easily hurt by teasing? — Are you easily offended or embarrassed, or is it like 'water off a duck's back'? — Are you easily embarrassed by the behavior of a significant other? — Do you believe that the healthier one's self-esteem, the less defensively they will handle teasing & criticism?)

367. **TECHNOLOGY: To what degree does your life involve smart technology? — A.** very much, **B.** somewhat, **C.** hardly at all ....A-B-C / NI-PC-DB
➤ (smart home products — voice activated smart speakers — smart gadgets — digital assistants — smart phones — other)

368. **TECHNOLOGY: Regarding technology, do you — A.** need to have the best & latest, **B.** want to have the best & latest, **C.** satisfied if it continues to do what it was purchased for, **D.** wait till it's obsolete? ....
....A-B-C D / NI-PC-DB
➤ (If money were no object, would your answer change?)

369. **THIRD-WORLD COUNTRIES: Are you concerned about violations of international human rights? — A.** very, **B.** somewhat, **C.** hardly at all ....A-B-C / NI-PC-DB
➤ (What should we do about despotic governments that violate these rights?)

— Miscellaneous —

370. **TELEMARKETERS: What's your attitude toward robocalls & live telemarking calls?** — **A.** hate them, **B.** screen them, **C.** ignore them, **D.** list them on the Do Not Call Registry list, **E.** block them, **F.** interested in some..**A-B-C-D-E-F / NI-PC-DB**
➤ (Which of these FTC complaint topics interest you? — reducing debt — vacation & timeshares — warranties & protection plans — medical & prescriptions — energy, solar & utilities — computer & tech support — home security & alarms — lotteries, prizes & sweepstakes — home improvement & cleaning — work from home — Do you feel vulnerable or susceptible to being taken by grifters, flimflammers, scammers & cheats? — Have you or someone you know ever been scammed?)

371. **THOUGHTS: Currently, what percent of the thoughts that occupy your mind are preoccupations, meaning they dominate or demand your attention, unwelcomed, vs. those thoughts that are there by 'choice & will'?** — **A.** a great percent, **B.** a large percent, **C.** a moderate percent, **D.** a small percent? ....
....**A-B-C-D / NI-PC-DB**
➤ (How much of your time is focused on wants vs. needs? — How much of your thinking time deals with worries & preoccupations vs. desires or exciting goals & plans?)

372. **TICKLING: Do you** — **A.** like being tickled, **B.** don't like it?..**A-B / NI-PC-DB**

373. **TIPPING: Do you consider yourself** — **A.** a generous tipper, **B.** a fair tipper, **C.** a non-tipper? ....**A-B-C / NI-PC-DB**
➤ (What's your attitude toward tip jars on counters? — How do you respond when a server stands over you while you're calculating the tip & completing your credit card charge? — Is tipping a productive custom? — How does tipping affect wage rates? — Should all tips be shared equally?)

— Miscellaneous —

374. **TRADE-OFFS: Every decision involves trade-offs.**
....**T-F / NI-PC-DB**

375. **TRANSPORTATION: How do you get around?** ....
....**NI-PC-DB**
➤ (car — motorcycle — bicycle — scooter — public transportation — driver — walk — skate board — Segue — friends — family — car pool — taxi — Uber — Lyft — other)

376. **TREATMENT OF SERVICE EMPLOYEES: How do you treat service employees? — A. kindly & considerately, B. disdainfully & condescendingly** ....**A-B / NI-PC-DB**
➤ (waitpersons — hotel employees — maids — baggage carriers — sales clerks — etc. — How do you view people who treat them poorly?)

377. **TROLLING: Is trolling, meaning the posting of inflammatory or inappropriate messages or comments online for the purpose of upsetting other users & provoking a response — A. harassment, intolerable & childish, B. unavoidable & unstoppable, C. potentially illegal, D. just fun?** ....**A-B-C-D / NI-PC-DB**

378. **UNDERWEAR: Do you wear — A. boxer shorts, B. briefs, C. go commando, D. panties, E. thongs, F. bikinis?** ....**A-B-C-D-E-F / NI-PC-DB**

379. **WAITING ROOMS: In waiting rooms, do you prefer — A. music, B. TV, C. silence?** ....**A-B-C / NI-PC-DB**

380. **WARNINGS: Can fear & pain serve a productive purpose?** ....**Y-N / NI-PC-DB**
➤ (At what point do they become unproductive?)

381. **WINNER: Everyone likes a winner but roots for the underdog.** ....**T-F / NI-PC-DB**

— Miscellaneous —

382. WOMEN'S LIB: What's your attitude toward the ERA ....
....NI-PC-DB
➤ (feminism — equity feminists — protesting for women's rights — NOW — Planned Parenthood)

383. WORKPLACE: Should the workplace be scent-free? ....
....Y-N / NI-PC-DB

384. WORKPLACE: Should the workplace be scent-free? ....
....Y-N / NI-PC-DB

385. UNIVERSE: Do you believe in the concept of multiverse or parallel universes? ....Y-N / NI-PC-DB

15. **MONEY, WORK, FINANCIAL**

Important! Please read.

TABLE OF CONTENTS — Page 5

23 Chapters Listed Alphabetically — 723 Main Questions —

Key words in each chapter are in alphabetical order for that chapter.

ANSWER CHOICES

Y-N (Yes No) — T-F (True False) — A-B-C (Multiple Choice)

NI (Non-Issue) — PC (Potential Conflict) — DB (Deal Breaker)

HOW TO ADDRESS THE QUESTIONS

Whether you're in a relationship or not, answer first for yourself, then ask yourself, how would you feel if your partner or a potential partner were to choose differently or the opposite? If reviewing with a partner and areas of disagreement arise, engage your sense of humor, remain calm, and discuss your differences civilly.

JUDGING AN ENTRY

Whatever you feel about an entry, be careful not to underestimate the value of what may appear to be a petty or trivial issue. You'd be surprised, or maybe not, at how little it can take to start an argument or reveal a major difference of opinion. A discussion of these minor issues can sometimes be quite revelatory..

RIGHT & WRONG

There are no absolutely right or wrong answers, just your subjective opinions expressed as a starting point for deliberation or discussion.

☆☆☆☆☆

— Money, Work & Financial —

386. **BANK ACCOUNTS: What's your attitude toward managing bank accounts?** ....NI-PC-DB
➤ (joint, separate or both — savings & checking — control of spending — commingling of funds & assets)

387. **BUSINESS: Who would you rather have as a business partner? — A. a best friend, B. a love interest, C. a spouse, D. an experienced business person, E. a recent business-school graduate, F. a relative?** ....
....A-B-C D-E F / NI-PC-DB

388. **CREDIT CARD: Would you ever put a cellphone service, or any large purchase for a friend with bad credit on your card?** ....Y-N / NI-PC-DB

389. **CREDIT & DEBIT CARDS: What's your attitude toward managing credit cards?** ....NI-PC-DB
➤ (rules for using them — payments late or on time — switching for better terms — pay minimums or balances monthly — one card or many)

390. **DEBT: Besides credit cards, what other debt are you carrying?** ....NI-PC-DB
➤ (home mortgage — auto loan — alimony — school loans — business loans — other — Are your payments late or on time? — Do you have plans to decrease your debt? — Is bankruptcy on the table?)

391. **FOCUS: Are you financially focused on — A. acquiring material things, B. frugality, C. living stress-free, D. saving for the future, E. getting off the grid or ghosting, F. getting rich & feeling financially secure** ....
....A-B-C-D-E-F / NI-PC-DB
➤ (Do you ever shop at Goodwill or the Salvation Army?)

— Money, Work & Financial —

392. INCOME: Do you have a stable income? ....Y-N / NI-PC-DB
➤ (Are you on a fixed income? — Is money no object or are you living month to month, week to week, or day to day? — Do you have a budget? — Would a large disparity in income with a partner be an issue? — Do you have goals & plans to increase your income potential? — If in a dead-end job, what is your solution to dealing with it?)

393. INVESTMENTS: Do you have investments? ....
....Y-N / NI-PC-DB
➤ (401 K — stocks or bonds — a pension — income property — own your own home — annuities — bitcoins, cryptocurrency, or blockchains)

394. MONEY: On a scale of 1 to 5, how important is money in your life? ....1-2-3-4-5 / NI-PC-DB
➤ (Assuming your basic needs are satisfied, what do you 'very-much-want' that more money could get you: new home — new car — freedom of choice — travel — romance — elective medical procedure — an employee — peace-of-mind — other? — Do you think wealthy people are statistically happier than most people?)

395. MONEY: How can you raise money? ....NI-PC-DB
➤ (borrow from banks — tap credit cards — open new cards — borrow from friends or relatives — solicit investors, **i.e.,** angels & venture capitalists — use guarantors or consignors — crowdfunding, **e.g.,** GoFundMe & Kickstarter — take on a partner — sell nonessential assets — downsize — get or refinance a mortgage — restructure debt — do a reverse mortgage — work overtime — get a second or part-time job — monetize a hobby — panhandle — ask for a raise — ask for an advance — sell your eggs, sperm, blood or body — get advance on inheritance — win the lottery — borrow from a loan shark — sell all or part of a life insurance policy — sell future income payments or structured settlements — gamble — become a Lyft or Uber driver — illegal activities, not recommended **e.g.,** rob a bank — sell drugs)

396. MONEY: Which do you most desire more of — A. money, B. time? ....A-B / NI-PC-DB

— Money, Work & Financial —

397. **MONEY: If you received an unexpected inheritance of $10,000, how would you spend the windfall?** ....
....**NI-PC-DB**
➤ (If money suddenly became no object, how would you spend your days?)

398. **MONEY: Money isn't everything.** ....**T-F / NI-PC-DB**
➤ (Have you ever passed on an opportunity to make more money in favor of a higher value or principle?)

399. **MONEY: How far would you be willing to go, illegally, for enough money to last a lifetime of luxury & freedom, if you knew you could never be caught?** .....
....**NI-PC-DB**
➤ (Would you kill a child molester? — Would you rob a bank? — Would you reveal military or state secrets? — At what point would your conscience become an issue?)

400. **PRENUP: Do you — A. want a prenup, B. don't want one, C. have one, D. deal breaker?** ......**A-B-C-D / NI-PC-DB**

401. **PROMOTION: Would you take a job promotion out of the area if it meant seeing your life partner only on weekends for a year or two?** ....**Y-N / NI-PC-DB**

402. **RETIREMENT: Are you retired or planning for it?** ....
....**Y-N / NI-PC-DB**
➤ (Have you done any estate planning? — Is the cost of college for your children covered? — Are you on social security? — Are your assets considered community property? — What will you do with your new found free time when you retire? — Can you imagine loving what you do & never wanting to retire?)

— Money, Work & Financial —

403. **RICH: Do you envy rich people?** ....Y-N / NI-PC-DB
➤ (Does your answer depend on how they got rich, **i.e.,** little life outside of work — little time for family — lied or cheated — engaged in underhanded, unscrupulous, behavior — really smart or highly educated — worked hard — inheritance — passionately loved their work?)

404. **RICH: What does it mean to be rich? — A.** enough money to never have to work again, **B.** enough money to be able to spend as much time as you want with those you love, **C.** enough money to buy any toy you want, **D.** enough money to afford spending your time doing what you love to do ....A-B-C-D / NI-PC-DB
➤ (Are you rich? — Do you expect to be rich? — When will you be rich? — How will you become rich?)

405. **SALES: Have you ever been involved in a multi-level sales organization?** ....Y-N / NI-PC-DB
➤ (Were you successful at it? — Did any of your friends make a living at it?)

406. **WORK: Most people work only out of necessity.** ....
....T-F- NI-PC-DB
➤ (If work is enjoyable, would you still call it work? — Is retirement a priority?)

407. **WORK: How many hours a day do you spend at work including getting ready for work plus travel time to & from work?** ....NI-PC-DB
➤ (How predictable is your work schedule? — Do your career, financial & work areas of life make it difficult to find a healthy balance with other-areas of life, **i.e.,** mental, physical, emotional, spiritual, social & family? — Given the choice, would you rather work from 10 to 7 or 7 to 4?)

— Money, Work & Financial —

408. WORK: Do you prefer that — A. both you & your partner work, **B.** one of you stays at home? ....**A-B / NI-PC-DB**
➤ (Does your answer depend on whether or not you have children? — Does it depend on your retirement goals?)

409. WORK: Are you considering a job change or relocation? ....**NI-PC-DB**
➤ (Is your resume up to date? — Will you get a letter of recommendation?)

410. WORK: What's your work situation? ....**NI-PC-DB**
➤ (Do you have, **e.g.,** a job — an occupation — a career — or own your own business? — Do you work full or part-time? — Do you have entrepreneurial aspirations? — Are you skilled or unskilled? — Are you unemployed due to technology or industry changes? — Are you looking for work or an internship? — Are you a creative artist? Are you artistic? — What's your work history?)

411. WORK: How can you avoid work? — A. win the lottery, **B.** love what you do ....**A-B / NI-PC-DB**

412. WORK: If you knew (don't ask how) you had only 10 years to live, would you stop working, if you had enough money to last 10 years? ....**Y-N / NI-PC-DB**

413. WORK: Is your work hard? ....**Y-N / NI-PC-DB**
➤ (What makes for a hard day's work, **e.g.,** laborious — always working against deadlines — emotionally unsatisfying — boring — financially unrewarding — feeling unappreciated — long hours — intellectually draining — on feet all day — no breaks — being under constant observation or supervision — not wanting to do it — no future — not good at it — feels meaningless — other?)

414. WORK: If money were no obstacle & you magically possessed or could acquire the requisite skills to do anything in life of your choosing, what would you like to do for a living, or for the pure joy of it? ....
....**NI-PC-DB**

— Money, Work & Financial —

415. **WORK: What would you do if you had a job that paid very well, offered great benefits, but your work environment had become so hostile & toxic due to favoritism, backstabbing & credit grabbing that it was having a negative affect on your personality & as a byproduct, on your relationship with your spouse & children?** ....NI-PC-DB

416. **WORK: How happy are you at work? — A. extremely happy, B. very happy, C. sufficiently happy, D. not very happy, E. very unhappy** ....**A-B-C D-E / NI-PC-DB**
➤ (Are you experiencing burn-out? — Is work stressful? — Is work more fulfilling than time spent away from work? — Do you have plans to improve your work situation? — Finish this proverb, "All work & no play makes Jack a___".)

417. **WORKING TOGETHER: What's your attitude about working with your partner?** ....NI-PC-DB
➤ (in your own business — at the same location — for the same company — in the same field of endeavor — How do you feel about sharing salary, pension & profit-sharing information with a partner?)

418. **WORRY: Do you worry that a robot — the internet — drones — self-driving vehicles — A.I. artificial intelligence — automation or other technology may someday make your job obsolete?** ....Y-N / NI-PC-DB
➤ (Are you taking steps to handle worst-case scenarios?)

419. **WORRY: Do you worry that you may someday lose your job to a younger worker?** ....Y-N / NI-PC-DB
➤ (How do feel about labor unions?)

16. __PERSONALITY & CHARACTER__

Important! Please read.

TABLE OF CONTENTS — Page 5

23 Chapters Listed Alphabetically — 723 Main Questions —

Key words in each chapter are in alphabetical order for that chapter.

ANSWER CHOICES

Y-N (Yes No) — T-F (True False) — A-B-C (Multiple Choice)

NI (Non-Issue) — PC (Potential Conflict) — DB (Deal Breaker)

HOW TO ADDRESS THE QUESTIONS

Whether you're in a relationship or not, answer first for yourself, then ask yourself, how would you feel if your partner or a potential partner were to choose differently or the opposite? If reviewing with a partner and areas of disagreement arise, engage your sense of humor, remain calm, and discuss your differences civilly.

JUDGING AN ENTRY

Whatever you feel about an entry, be careful not to underestimate the value of what may appear to be a petty or trivial issue. You'd be surprised, or maybe not, at how little it can take to start an argument or reveal a major difference of opinion. A discussion of these minor issues can sometimes be quite revelatory..

RIGHT & WRONG

There are no absolutely right or wrong answers, just your subjective opinions expressed as a starting point for deliberation or discussion.

☆☆☆☆☆

113 of 187

— Personality & Character —

420. **AMBITIOUS: Do you consider yourself ambitious, hardworking, driven?** ....Y-N / NI-PC-DB

421. **ANGRY: Have you ever been accused of being resentful, easily angered or annoyed?** ....Y-N / NI-PC-DB
➤ (Do you have a chip on your shoulder? — Do you tend to hold on to past slights? — Have you ever punched a mirror?)

422. **ANXIOUS: Do you consider yourself anxious, always , in a hurry & stressed out over small interruptions in your schedule or intrusions on you time?** ....
....Y-N / NI-PC-DB
➤ (Is your stress mostly externally imposed or self-imposed? — Are you familiar with the concept of eustress vs. distress? — If anxious, are you also a perfectionist & impatient? — Which came first? — How crowded is your lifestyle schedule? — Do you consider yourself hyperactive & energized or just anxious?)

423. **ARROGANT: Have you ever been accused of being arrogant, cocky, conceited, dogmatic, or egotistical?**
....Y-N / NI-PC-DB
➤ (Do you have a superiority complex? — Do you find it difficult to say, "I was wrong"? — How much concern do you have for what others think of you & your opinions?)

424. **APPEARANCE: Personality is affected by one's appearance. — A. strongly agree, B. agree, C. neutral, D. disagree, E. strongly disagree** ....A-B-C-D-E / NI-PC-DB
➤ (Are attractive people nicer than those less attractive?)

425. **ASSERTIVE: Do you consider yourself — A. assertive, B. aggressive, C. self-assured, D. neither?** ....
....A-B-C / NI-PC-DB
➤ (How do you distinguish between assertive & aggressive? — Do you have the confidence to speak truth to power or would you feel you're being insubordinate? — How many pushbacks against a "NO" turns assertive behavior into aggressive?)

— Personality & Character —

426. **BEHAVIOR: Can drug or alcohol use be a justifiable excuse for contemptible or disgraceful behavior?**......
....Y-N / NI-PC-DB

427. **BEHAVIOR: Have you ever been talked into doing something against your will?** ....NI-PC-DB
➤ (Do you ever do something you don't want to do just to please another person?)

428. **BEHAVIOR: Self-defeating urges & desires can be overridden by intelligence & awareness — A.** always, **B.** most of the time, **C.** often, **D.** sometimes, **E.** rarely......
....A-B-C-D-E / NI-PC-DB

429. **BEHAVIOR: The best predictor of future behavior is past behavior.** ....T-F / NI-PC-DB
➤ (Is who you are synonymous with who you were, or could become?)

430. **CALM: Are you calm, patient, easygoing & centered, even under deadlines?** ....Y-N / NI-PC-DB
➤ (Are you composed under stress & pressure? — Are you unlikely to panic in difficult situations, disasters & tragedies? — Are you easily frazzled & harried?)

431. **CEREMONY: Do you consider yourself as someone who — A. stands on ceremony, custom, convention, tradition, protocol, formality & norms, B. someone who often does not behave as expected by the majority?** .... A-B / NI-PC-DB
➤ (Do you follow trends? — Do you follow the crowd?)

— Personality & Character —

432. **CHANGE: Behavior is context driven. People change their behavior in response to changes in their conditions & circumstances, but seldom change their core personality, character, or temperament** ....T-F / NI-PC-DB

433. **CHANGE: You can't change other people's personality or their bad habits re: losing weight, drinking, drugs, or smoking, only they can.** ....T-F / NI-PC-DB

434. **CHANGE: You can't easily change your urges or desires, but you can choose to refrain from engaging in the undesirable behaviors they might trigger.** ....T-F / NI-PC-DB

435. **CHAUVINISTIC: Have you even been called chauvinistic, misogynistic, or misandristic?** ....Y-N / NI-PC-DB
   ➤ (Are you offended by those who are?)

436. **CHILDISH: Have you ever been accused of being infantile & adolescent vs. mature & adult?** ....Y-N / NI-PC-DB
   ➤ (Have you ever been called needy?)

437. **COMPLIMENT: Which compliment or praise would you most like to hear? — A. you have a great heart & an incredible personality, B. you have a brilliant mind & extraordinary judgment, C. you are exceptionally creative & incomparably talented, D. you are extremely disciplined & hard-working, E. you are dependable, responsible & trustworthy, F. you are beautiful, handsome, very attractive** ....A-B-C-D-E-F / NI-PC-DB
   ➤ (Has positive feedback from a respected source ever profoundly affected your life choices or self-image? — Is talent that is not used to its fullest the same as wasted talent?)

— Personality & Character —

438. **CONTROLLING: Have you ever been accused of being controlling?** ....Y-N / NI-PC-DB
➤ (Ever been called a control freak, bossy, authoritarian, overbearing, dictatorial, or tyrannical, vs. flexible & yielding? — Do you nag & badger to motivate behavioral changes in others? — Do you agree with the idea that thinking you're in control is often an illusion of ego? — Do you ever feel out of control? — How important is it to feel in control? — Do you aspire to be boss?)

439. **CREATIVE: Do you consider yourself creative, inventive & resourceful vs. unimaginative & un-resourceful?** ....Y-N / NI-PC-DB
➤ (Are you using your creative talents?)

440. **CREATURE OF HABIT: Do your habitual life patterns have you stuck in a rut?** ....Y-N / NI-PC-DB
➤ (Do you foresee your life changing in any significant way during the next five years? — Do you have any plans or goals to improve what's right with your life, or change what's wrong with it?)

441. **CURIOSITY: Do you consider yourself curious & inquisitive about many things?** ....Y-N / NI-PC-DB
➤ (When something happens that makes no sense, a lost item or a weird occurrence, do you feel pressed to resolve your curiosity, or are you quick to let it go? Do you have a reputation for asking a lot of questions?

442. **CYNICAL: Have you ever been accused of being cynical?** ....Y-N / NI-PC-DB
➤ (Do you usually assume the worst about people's true motivations? — Do you have a cynical & pessimistic view about life & the future? — Do you believe in the promises made by politicians or the agendas professed by the government? — Do you hesitate to believe hyperbolic claims made by companies, **e.g.,** the Theranos, Elizabeth Holmes, blood-testing fraud?)

— Personality & Character —

443. **DAREDEVIL: Do you consider yourself a daredevil, an adrenaline junkie, a risk-taker?** ....Y-N / NI-PC-DB
➤ (Do you like challenging, dangerous sports, **e.g.,** skydiving — hang gliding — bungee jumping — rock climbing — surfing big waves — running with the bulls — running the rapids — base-jumping — snow boarding down mountains — moto-crossing on mountain ridges, etc. — Do first responders, **i.e.,** fire, police, rescue & medical fall into this category? — Is danger stressful if you're used to it? — Can a person who likes being in control also be a risk-taker? — Can a person be a financial & emotional risk-taker while not being a physical thrill-seeker? — How do you feel about roller coasters? — Could you be an embedded war correspondent?)

444. **DOMINANT: Do you consider yourself — A.
domineering, B. submissive, C. balanced?**......................
....A-B-C / NI-PC-DB

445. **DRAMATIC: Have you ever been accused of being a drama queen or king?** ....Y-N / NI-PC-DB
➤ (Do you make mountains out of molehills, a big deal out of, **e.g.,** petty issues, annoying situations & little hassles? — Do you react to minor problems as tragedies, disasters & catastrophes?—Are you a medical alarmist? — Are you a catastrophizer?)

446. **EMOTIONAL: Are you particularly emotional?** ....
....Y-N / NI-PC-DB
➤ (How often do you experience a strong emotional state of, **e.g.,** fear — hate — anger — resentment — anxiety — depression — love — joy — excitement — envy — jealousy — emotionally neutral at homeostasis —needy?)

— *Personality & Character* —

447. **ETIQUETTE: Do you consider yourself polite, tactful & mannerly?** ....Y-N / NI-PC-DB
➤ (How important to you are right & wrong, manners, etiquette & propriety? — Do you always say thank you & please? — How do you feel about social etiquette, **e.g.,** double dipping — drinking from soda bottle or milk cartoon — burping — passing gas — wiping feet when entering a home — eating with mouth open — texting or using a cellphone at dinner, in a restaurant, or movie theater — wearing a hat indoors — standing when someone enters the room — excusing yourself when sneezing — opening car doors for your passenger — interjecting vs. interrupting a speaker — thank you for a gift by phone or text, etc.

448. **EXAGGERATOR: Have you ever been accused of being an inveterate or compulsive exaggerator? Are you prone to hyperbole & the misuse or overuse of absolutes & gross exaggerations?** ....Y-N / NI-PC-DB

449. **FAULTS: Have you ever been accused of being honest to a fault, loyal to a fault, or generous to a fault?** ....
....Y-N / NI-PC-DB

450. **FEISTY: Do you consider yourself fiery, excitable, lively, gutsy & spirited?** ....Y-N / NI-PC-DB

451. **FINANCIAL STATUS: Personality is affected by one's financial status.** — **A.** strongly agree, **B.** agree, **C.** neutral, **D.** disagree, **E.** strongly disagree ....
....A-B-C-D-E / NI-PC-DB
➤ (Statistically who has a nicer personality, rich people or poor people?)

452. **FLEXIBLE: Do you consider yourself flexible, adaptable & easy-going?** ....Y-N / NI-PC-DB
➤ (How do you respond to inflexible, 'black & white' thinking?)

— Personality & Character —

453. FREE SPIRITED: Do you reject established institutions? ....Y-N / NI-PC-DB
➤ (Do you consider yourself 'hippy-like'?)

454. GAME PLAYER: Have you ever been accused of being a game player? ....Y-N / NI-PC-DB
➤ (Have you been accused of being secretive, deceitful, or duplicitous? — Do your words match your actions? — Do you engage in mind games?)

455. GEEKY & NERDY: Have you ever been called a geek or a nerd? ....Y-N / NI-PC-DB
➤ (Do you see yourself as smart, but not very 'cool'?)

456. GOOD PERSON: Do you consider yourself a good person, always trying to do the right thing? ....
....Y-N / NI-PC-DB

457. GRACIOUS: Do you consider yourself a gracious person? ....Y-N / NI-PC-DB
➤ (Do you have a habit of expressing gratitude? — Do you always send thank you notes? — Do you have a count-your-blessings list?)

458. HAPPY: Are you basically an upbeat, happy person? ..
....Y-N / NI-PC-DB
➤ (Are you not easily taken off your game? — Do you enjoy cartoons?)

459. HEALTH: Personality is affected by one's state of health. — A. strongly agree, B. agree, C. neutral, D. disagree, E. strongly disagree ....A-B-C-D-E / NI-PC-DB
➤ (Do you remain pleasant even when troubled with health issues?)

— Personality & Character —

460. HELPFUL: Do you consider yourself a helpful person?
....Y-N / NI-PC-DB

➤ (Do you help people enjoy themselves through entertainment, the arts, or humor? — Do you help people make, save or manage their money? — Do you help people make intelligent thoughtful decisions? — Do you comfort people? — Do you help people solve problems? — Do you help people get, be, or stay healthy? — Do you help people just for the joy & satisfaction of being helpful, or mainly in exchange for compensation, or to earn a living? — Does being helpful make you feel good? — If you didn't feel good about helping, would you help? — Have you ever helped someone move? — Ever been told you changed or saved someone's life with your printed or spoken words? — Have you ever house-sat for someone's dog, or cat? — Ever watered someone's plants or lawn while they were away? — Ever taken food to the ill, or sent money to a charity? — Ever taken someone to or picked someone up from the airport? — Do you believe most people have a mission to help others? — Are you in a helping profession or first-responder occupation? — Would you like to be known as a hero? — Would you like credit for saving or improving people's lives? — Is your goal to make the world a better place because you were here? — Is Mother Theresa a 'her-o' of yours? — Would you rather be a live coward or a dead hero?)

461. HUMOROUS: Do you consider yourself humorous, amusing, entertaining & witty?.................Y-N / NI-PC-DB

➤ (Can you laugh at yourself, **i.e.**, your shortcomings, foibles, mistakes & failures? — Do you have a good sense of humor?)

462. INCONSIDERATE: Have you ever been accused of being inconsiderate or insensitive to others' feelings or needs? ....Y-N / NI-PC-DB

463. INDEPENDENT: Do you consider yourself independent, self-reliant & self-sufficient, with little concern for what others think, say, or do? ....
....Y-N / NI-PC-DB

— Personality & Character —

464. **INTELLIGENCE: Personality is affected by one's level of intelligence?** — **A.** strongly agree, **B.** agree, **C.** neutral, **D.** disagree, **E.** strongly disagree ....
....**A-B-C-D-E / NI-PC-DB**
➤ (Statistically who has a nicer personality, better educated or less educated people?)

465. **JEALOUS: Have you ever been accused of being jealous, possessive, insecure, clingy, or stroke deprived?** ....**Y-N / NI-PC-DB**
➤ (Do you need proof that you're loved & lovable? — Do you crave attention? — Do you have a strong affiliation need for approval & acceptance? — Do you always need to have people around?)

466. **JOKESTER: Have you ever been called a jokester?** .....
....**Y-N / NI-PC-DB**
➤ (Are you always telling jokes, including off-color jokes in mixed company?)

467. **JUDGMENTAL: Have you ever been accused of being judgmental, righteous, or smugly moralistic?** ....
....**Y-N / NI-PC-DB**
➤ (Do you feel or communicate that you're better than or smarter than others? — Do you appear snobbish, pompous, or elitist? — Are you class conscious? — Do you have rigid or strict rules about morality or the right & wrong way to behave? — Do you ever judge people by their choice of music, movies, or their TV favorites? — Are you quick to set people straight?)

468. **KLUTZY: Have you ever been called klutzy or clumsy?**
....**Y-N / NI-PC-DB**
➤ (Do you drop things or fall down more often than you'd like?)

469. **LEADER: Do you consider yourself a leader?** ....
....**Y-N / NI-PC-DB**
➤ (Are you an initiator, the one who gets things going, a motivator who inspires followers? — Should leaders make friends with followers or maintain a professional distance?)

— Personality & Character —

470. **LITIGIOUS: Are you quick to sue?** ....Y-N / NI-PC-DB

471. **LOVING & CARING: Do you consider yourself loving & caring, supportive & understanding, sympathetic & empathetic, nurturing?** ....Y-N / NI-PC-DB
➤ (Are you sensitive, kind & compassionate? — Do you instinctively reach out to people who are hurting or in need? — Do you catch spiders & release them outside?

472. **MAKING IT HAPPEN: Do you consider yourself a goal-directed, 'making it happen' kind of person vs. having more of a 'laissez-faire, que sera, sera' attitude?** ....Y-N / NI-PC-DB

473. **MATURE: Do you consider yourself mature & responsible?**..Y-N / NI-PC-DB
➤ (Are you ever accused of being immature, childlike & irresponsible, or needy?

474. **METICULOUS: Do you consider yourself meticulous, very detail oriented?** ....Y-N / NI-PC-DB
➤ (Do you value precision & accuracy? — Do you like having a place for everything & everything in its place? — Do you consider yourself perfectionistic, even fussy & fastidious? — Are you frivolous?)

475. **MOODY: Have you ever been accused of being moody, depressive & downbeat vs. basically happy?**..............
....Y-N / NI-PC-DB
➤ (When moody, do you avoid people or reach out hoping they'll bring you out of your funk?)

— Personality & Character —

476. **MOTIVATED: Do you consider yourself motivated & goal-directed vs. having little ambition?** ....
....Y-N / NI-PC-DB
➤ (Are you positively motivated vs. fear motivated? — Which motivates you more, your wants or your needs? — Do you have goals, plans, dreams, or fantasies that motivate & excite you? — Which is the stronger motivator, fear or reward? — Which goals are more motivational, short-term or long-term? — What percent of your day is spent in need-to-do's, have-to-do's & should-do's vs. want-to's? — Do you agree that many important decisions are based not on single issues, but rather, they are complicated by multiple motivators: pros vs. cons — needs vs. wants — fears vs. desires?)

477. **NARCISSISTIC: Have you ever been called narcissistic, self-centered, self-absorbed, egotistical, or self-important?** ....Y-N / NI-PC-DB
➤ (When does narcissism earn the 'narcissistic personality disorder' label?)

478. **NATURE LOVER: Do you consider yourself an outdoorsy, camping enthusiast vs. a homebody who prefers modern conveniences?** ....Y-N / NI-PC-DB

479. **OBSESSIVE-COMPULSIVE: Have you ever been accused of being obsessive-compulsive?** ....
....Y-N / NI-PC-DB
➤ (Are you neurotically perfectionistic & indecisive? — Do you have recurring unwanted thoughts, or perform certain routines repeatedly?

480. **OPTIMISTIC: Do you consider yourself optimistic, positive & enthusiastic?** ....Y-N / NI-PC-DB
➤ (Are you sometimes accused of seeing life through rose-colored glasses? — Are you an upbeat vs. downbeat kind of person? — Do you believe it's never too late to believe in dreams?)

— Personality & Character —

481. **ORGANIZED: Do you consider yourself organized & orderly, not messy?** ....Y-N / NI-PC-DB
➤ (Do you keep the following neat & tidy, **e.g.,** your desk — work space — closets — drawers — kitchen — car? — Are you into domestic chores? — Is your time organized? — Are you prepared for emergencies & natural disasters? — Can you quickly put your hands on important papers, **e.g.,** insurance policies — titles — investments — will — stock certificates? —How accessible are important phone numbers, **e.g.,** medical — attorney — bank — & emergency contacts? — miscellaneous, **e.g.,** off-premise storage facilities — list of medications — health directives — location of heirlooms, jewelry, antiques & collectibles — Are your tools organized & handy? — Do you clean up & care for your tools after repair projects? — Have you ever been called either 'fastidious' or a 'slob'?)

482. **PACK RAT: Have you ever been called a pack-rat, a hoarder who stores almost anything & everything & discards almost nothing?** ....Y-N / NI-PC-DB
➤ (If you use what you hoard, can you find items when you need them? — What distinguishes a hoarder from a collector?)

483. **PARANOID: Have you ever been accused of being paranoid?**..Y-N / NI-PC-DB
➤ (Are you preoccupied with an invasion of your privacy, doing business online, or government intrusion? — Do you have an irrational distrust of people's motives & intentions? — Do you consider yourself basically fearful?)

484. **PASSIONATE: Do you consider yourself a passionate soul? Are you driven, fervent & ardent about many things, a dream chaser, intensely devoted?** ....
....Y-N / NI-PC-DB
➤ (What do you feel most passionate about?)

— Personality & Character —

485. PASSIVE-AGGRESSIVE: Have you ever been accused of being passive-aggressive vs. straight-forward? .....
....Y-N / NI-PC-DB
➤ (Do you use subtle sarcasm to communicate unexpressed hurt or anger? — Do you express hostility indirectly through procrastination, stubbornness, sullen behavior, or stone-cold silence? — Is your tone often inconsistent with your spoken words?)

486. PERSONALITY: On a scale of 1 to 5, how important is personality in judging a partner? ......1-2-3-4-5 / NI-PC-DB
➤ (In 10 individual words, how would define your personality? — Have you ever considered that what you consider to be your greatest weakness may be your greatest strength? — What top 5 personality or character traits would you most like to be an example of?)

487. PRACTICAL: Do you consider yourself practical, pragmatic & realistic? ....Y-N / NI-PC-DB
➤ (Do others ever call you impractical, unrealistic, or an idealist?)

488. PRANKSTER: Have you ever been called a prankster, always playing tricks & practical jokes on others?.....
....Y-N / NI-PC-DB

489. PRIDE & HUMILITY: Which character trait most reflects your personality? — A. prideful, B. humble
....A-B / NI-PC-DB
➤ (Is pride a sin? — Is it a sin to be proud of your accomplishments or those of loved ones? — Is it a sin to be proud of yourself for living up to your word & giving up your bad habits? — Have you ever swallowed your pride? — When does pride become arrogance?)

490. PROCRASTINATOR: Have you ever been called a procrastinator? ....Y-N / NI-PC-DB
➤ (Do you have a tendency to put off doing things you don't want to do, even if they need to be done? — Do you also put off doing things you say you'd like to do, but your to-do list is too long?)

— Personality & Character —

491. **PUNCTUAL: Do you consider yourself punctual, almost always on time?**............................Y-N / NI-PC-DB
➤ (Are you dependable & reliable or often late without a reasonable explanation? — Does being late make you feel guilty? — Is being 'in time' different from being 'on-time'?)

492. **QUICK: Can a person be a potential love interest if they are: quick to show a temper — quick to take offense — quick to disagree — quick to judge or criticize — quick to be pessimistic — quick to defend their theories & opinions as fact — quick to make mountains out of molehills — quick to get even when slighted?**..................................Y-N / NI-PC-DB

493. **RESCUER: Have you ever been called a rescuer or savior?** ....Y-N / NI-PC-DB
➤ (Are you motivated to help people solve their personal problems? — Do you have a need to be needed? — Is your self-esteem tied to your rescues? — Do you regularly search for sympathetic victims to rescue? — Are you an enabler?)

494. **RESENTFUL: Have you ever been accused of being resentful, a grudge holder, slow to forget grievances & slights, vs. quick to forgive?** ....Y-N / NI-PC-DB

495. **ROMANTIC: Do you consider yourself romantic & sentimental?** ....Y-N / NI-PC-DB
➤ (Do you sometimes express strong feelings of love, happiness, sadness, pity, nostalgia in a way that may seem to others as foolish, excessive, or gushy? — Which is more emotionally satisfying, being in love or being loved?)

496. **SARCASTIC: ,Have you ever been accused of being sarcastic, mean & insulting?** ....Y-N / NI-PC-DB
➤ (Do you use remarks that clearly mean the opposite of what you say in order to hurt or put others down? — Do you consider sarcasm as being witty & anyone who can't handle it can't take a joke?)

— Personality & Character —

497. SELF-CONFIDENT: Do you consider yourself self-confident with a strong & healthy ego?......................
....Y-N / NI-PC-DB
➤ (Do you believe strongly in your abilities, capabilities & potential? — Do you brag or boast about them?)

498. SELF-DISCIPLINED: Do you consider yourself self-disciplined & self-controlled?...................Y-N / NI-PC-DB
➤ (Are you methodical & capable of great focus? — How comfortable are you with deferred gratification?)

499. SELF-ESTEEM: Do you believe that true self-esteem can be achieved or raised with business success, cosmetic surgery, or by being married to a high profile, famous partner?...........................Y-N / NI-PC-DB

500. SELF-ESTEEM: Do you consider yourself as having healthy self-esteem & an accurate self-image?...........
....Y-N / NI-PC-DB
➤ (Do you have direct self-acceptance vs. indirect self-acceptance based on the approval of others? — Are you or are you not easily humiliated or embarrassed? — Are you or are you not reactive, defensive, or overly sensitive to slights, criticism, name calling, or teasing? —How easily are your feelings hurt when your character is judged harshly — Do you believe in 'sticks & stones may break your bones, but names will never hurt you, unless you let them'? — How would you respond to being called unstable, inept, inexperienced or unethical? — If you were called stupid, would you respond defensively? — Would you be less defensive if told you were acting stupid or talking stupid?)

501. SELF-ESTEEM: Is boastful self-confidence, cockiness, or egotistical expressions of superiority evidence of high self-esteem?.......................................Y-N / NI-PC-DB
➤ (Does the statement 'It's not bragging if it's true' affect your answer? — Can you explain the difference between self-esteem & self-confidence? — Is being pretentious a sign of low self-esteem?)

— *Personality & Character* —

502. **SELF-ESTEEM: Low self-esteem is maybe our greatest obstacle to happiness & fulfillment.** ....
....T-F / NI-PC-DB

503. **SKEPTICAL: Do you consider yourself skeptical & cautious, slow & hesitant to believe disparate, diverse things?** ....Y-N / NI-PC-DB
➤ (Would you call yourself a 'doubting Thomas or simply highly enlightened & aware?

504. **SOCIABLE: Do you consider yourself sociable & charming, outgoing & extroverted?** ....Y-N / NI-PC-DB
➤ (Ever been called boring, introverted, shy & reclusive?)

505. **SQUEAMISH: Have you ever been accused of being squeamish, easily grossed out, shocked, nauseated, or disgusted?** ....Y-N / NI-PC-DB
➤ (blood — vomit —poop —needles — description of medical procedures — naked-very fat people at nude beaches — other)

506. **STUBBORN: Have you ever been accused of being stubborn, obstinate, inflexible & opinionated?**............
....Y-N / NI-PC-DB
➤ (Do you express your opinions & feelings as though they were facts? — Do you defensively resist deviation from your established views, perspectives, schedules & routines? — Can you listen non-defensively & non-reactively to opposing opinions?)

507. **SUPERSTITIOUS: Do you consider yourself superstitious?** ....Y-N / NI-PC-DB
➤ (Friday the 13th — walking under a ladder — stepping on a crack — breaking a mirror — black cat crossing — full moon — other — How often do you experience evidence of their validity?)

— Personality & Character —

508. **TALKER: Have you ever been called a talker, a poor listener who interrupts, but can't be interrupted?** ....
....Y-N / NI-PC-DB
➤ (Are there times when interrupting is justifiable?)

509. **TEMPERAMENTAL: Have you ever been accused of being temperamental?** ....Y-N / NI-PC-DB
➤ (Have you been accused of being short tempered, having a short fuse, lacking impulse control or labeled intense — wired — a tight ass — high strung — defensive — or thin-skinned? — Are you easily provoked — emotionally explosive — reactive to criticism, differences of opinion, or a critique of your character flaws? — If you were to act as a mediator in an argument between friends, would you be viewed as having a judicial temperament? — Have you ever been in a fight? — At what age? — Have you ever lost relationships over any of these traits?)

510. **TRUSTING: Do you consider yourself an inherently trusting person?** ....Y-N / NI-PC-DB
➤ (Has your trust ever been misplaced or met with betrayal? — Have you ever been called naive, gullible & too trusting — Do you trust anyone more than yourself?)

511. **TRUSTING: How would you respond to a betrayal of trust? — A. never speak to the betrayer again, B. always feel resentful & distrustful, C. wish them bad karma, D. find a way to get revenge, E. with forgiveness, if sufficiently satisfied with their explanation & genuine remorse** ....A-B-C-D-E / NI-PC-DB

512. **TRUSTWORTHY: Do you consider yourself honest & trustworthy, sincere & open?** ....Y-N / NI-PC-DB
➤ (Do you exude integrity? — Does sharing intimate feelings, including faults & admissions against your self-interest make you more trustworthy? — Do you consider yourself authentic, genuine, real, a straight shooter? — How honest are your answers to the questions throughout this checklist? — How important is your word & your credibility?)

— Personality & Character —

513. **TYPE A: Do you consider yourself a Type A personality, very competitive & driven?** ....
....Y-N / NI-PC-DB
➤ (Are you motivated by a need to win or a preference to win? — Does being recognized as the best at something motivate you? — Would you rather win an award for being the star of a team or for being the most outstanding team player?)

514. **UNPREDICTABLE: Have you ever been accused of being unpredictable, impulsive, inconsistent?** ....
....Y-N / NI-PC-DB
➤ (Do you change attitudes & behaviors without warning? — Does being unpredictable make a person more interesting & exciting or untrustworthy?)

515. **VENGEFUL: Have you ever been accused of being vengeful, vindictive, punitive & retaliative, always wanting to get even vs. forgiving?** ....Y-N / NI-PC-DB
➤ (Can vengeance in the form of violence ever be justified? — Is vengeance in the name of God rational?)

516. **VICTIM: Have you ever been told that you have a self-pitying, "poor-me" attitude?** ....Y-N / NI-PC-DB
➤ (Do you think the world is working against you? — Have you ever been called a 'complainer'?)

517. **WEIRD: Do you ever say, 'people are weird'?** ....
....Y-N / NI-PC-DB
➤ (Does this apply to you, also? — Would you rather be called weird, unique, special, or different?)

518. **WINNER: Do you consider yourself a winner?** ....
....Y-N / NI-PC-DB
➤ (What have you won or succeeded at that made you feel proud of yourself? — Have you ever received any awards or trophies? — Is there someone, in particular, that you would want to be proud of you or your accomplishments?)

— Personality & Character —

519. **WIRING: Is one's mental 'wiring' re: defensiveness & reactiveness more a function of — A.** genetics, **B.** one's thinking & attitudes, **C.** one's conditioning & upbringing?...A-B-C / NI-PC-DB

520. **WORTHLESS: Have you ever been told that you were worthless or a disappointment?**...............Y-N / NI-PC-DB
➤ (Has it had any lasting effect on your personality?)

521. **WORRIER: Have you ever been told that you're a worrier?**..Y-N / NI-PC-DB
➤ (Are you always concerned that things either are not going to improve, or are going to get worse? — Are you a defeatist inclined to become overwhelmed & have melt-downs when things aren't going your way?)

522. **YOURSELF: Is 'be yourself' — A.** good advice, **B.** bad or useless advice, **C.** depends? ....A-B-C / NI-PC-DB

17. <u>PHILOSOPHY</u>

Rodin's 'The Thinker'

<u>*Important! Please read.*</u>

<u>TABLE OF CONTENTS</u> — Page 5

23 Chapters Listed Alphabetically — 723 Main Questions —

Key words in each chapter are in alphabetical order for that chapter.

<u>ANSWER CHOICES</u>

Y-N (Yes No) — T-F (True False) — A-B-C (Multiple Choice)

NI (Non-Issue) — PC (Potential Conflict) — DB (Deal Breaker)

<u>HOW TO ADDRESS THE QUESTIONS</u>

Whether you're in a relationship or not, answer first for yourself, then ask yourself, how would you feel if your partner or a potential partner were to choose differently or the opposite? If reviewing with a partner and areas of disagreement arise, engage your sense of humor, remain calm, and discuss your differences civilly.

<u>JUDGING AN ENTRY</u>

Whatever you feel about an entry, be careful not to underestimate the value of what may appear to be a petty or trivial issue. You'd be surprised, or maybe not, at how little it can take to start an argument or reveal a major difference of opinion. A discussion of these minor issues can sometimes be quite revelatory..

<u>RIGHT & WRONG</u>

There are no absolutely right or wrong answers, just your subjective opinions expressed as a starting point for deliberation or discussion.

☆☆☆☆☆

— Philosophy —

523. ACCIDENTS: There are no accidents. ....T-F / NI-PC-DB
➤ (Is it true or false that there are no coincidences?

524. ATTITUDE: Can the attitude of 'good enough' be an obstacle to excellence? ....Y-N / NI-PC-DB
➤ (Can aiming for perfection improve the odds of achieving excellence? — Can aiming for the stars help you reach the moon? — Does demanding perfection of yourself make the achievement of excellence less rewarding? — Do you see perfectionism as a form of self-abuse?)

525. BELIEFS: What does it say about your values, principles & philosophical beliefs regarding life, if they are not reflected in either your actions or your emotional state of mind, despite professing or declaring them out loud to others? ....NI-PC-DB
➤ (Does the word hypocrisy jump out? — Are your beliefs evidenced in your actions & behavior?—Do you consider yourself a person of integrity? — Are you who you say you are, or do you suffer from the 'imposter syndrome'?)

526. BIAS: Is it human nature to view the world through selective perception? ....Y-N / NI-PC-DB
➤ (Do we all have confirmation biases, conscious & unconscious? — Does this mean we all tend to selectively see, hear & accept evidence that supports & confirms our preconceived notions, while evidence that contradicts or conflicts with our current positions is often doubted or even ignored? — Does this human tendency explain our disinclination to admit when we are wrong?)

527. CAUSES: What does it mean when we say, "everything happens for a reason"? ....NI-PC-DB
➤ (Who determines the reason? — Through what thought process do you ascribe or attribute causes to events?)

528. CHOICE: Have you ever made a life-impacting decision that felt like either a choice between 'the lesser of evils,' or no choice at all? ....Y-N / NI-PC-DB

— Philosophy —

529. **CHOICE: Would you rather — <u>A.</u> serve in heaven, <u>B.</u> reign in hell?** ....A-B / NI-PC-DB

530. **CHEEK: 'Turn the other cheek' is better than the alternatives.** ....T-F / NI-PC-DB
    ➤ (What are the alternatives?)

531. **CHICKENS: Is your behavior ever influenced by the phrase, 'don't count your chickens before they're hatched'?** ....Y-N / NI-PC-DB
    ➤ (Does this phrase downplay optimism?)

532. **DISAPPOINTMENTS: Disappointments are inevitable, but discouragement is both a choice & an attitude.**.....
    ....T-F / NI-PC-DB
    ➤ (Do you believe that viewing disappointments as learning experiences makes the disappointment easier to accept & by focusing on the bright side, looking for the silver lining, the Felix culpa, or blessing in disguise, a disappointment can be changed to a positive experience in the blink of an eye? — Is lowering your expectations an effective way to cut down on disappointments? — Is it best to expect little & be pleasantly surprised? — What is the downside of having low expectations? — Can meaning be found in tragedy & great disappointments?)

533. **ENVELOPE: When it comes to pushing the envelope, do you believe in the idea, 'you can never know how far you can go until you've gone too far'?** ....
    ....Y-N / NI-PC-DB

— *Philosophy* —

534. **FAILURE: Does a single mistake make you a mistake; does a single failure, make you a failure?**.....................
....Y-N / NI-PC-DB
➤ (How many mistakes & failures are you allowed before you find it difficult to shake the label? — Who's the judge of your efforts & results? — Who's the scorekeeper? — What's the difference between a setback, a learning experience & a failure?—How many times did Thomas Edison fail before he created the incandescent light bulb; how many elections did Abraham Lincoln lose before he became president; how many times did Babe Ruth strike out before setting his hitting records?)

535. **FAKE IT: Is the attitude, 'fake it till you make it' a good philosophy?**...Y-N / NI-PC-DB

536. **FEELINGS: The major cause of your feelings is — A. a function of what & how you think, B. caused by others & how they treat you, C. a reaction to your experiences & circumstances, D. other**........................A-B-C-D / NI-PC-DB
➤ (Can you change your feelings by changing your thoughts? — Can you control your thoughts? — Do you agree with the premise, 'GIGO' — garbage in, garbage out? — Have you ever said, "I can't help how I feel, or you make me feel so angry"?)

537. **FEELINGS: Is the attitude 'if it feels good, do it' a good philosophy?**...Y-N / NI-PC-DB

538. **FEELINGS: We all enjoy 'feeling' the following:** ....
....T-F / NI-PC-DB
➤ (good about ourselves — special — unique — important — valued — appreciated — useful — loved — accepted — respected — understood — trusted — admired — liked — Do you agree that the ability to sincerely help people feel this way is also helpful in making friends & influencing people?)

— Philosophy —

539. **FEELINGS: You can't control your feelings or how you feel.** ....T-F / NI-PC-DB
➤ (Can you control your thoughts? — Are your thoughts related to your feelings?)

540. **FOREVER: Does anything last forever?** .....Y-N / NI-PC-DB
➤ (Does anything last a lifetime?)

541. **FRAUD: Everyone sometimes feels like a fraud?** ....
....T-F / NI-PC-DB
➤ (Is a fraud generally a hypocrite, also?)

542. **GOOD: There's good in everyone.** ....T-F / NI-PC-DB

543. **HAPPINESS: Is happiness more — A.** a matter of mind, **B.** a function of conditions & circumstances? ....
....A-B / NI-PC-DB
➤ (Can you be happy without peace of mind? — Can you have peace of mind when you're preoccupied with problems that demand attention until resolved? — Can you have peace of mind & be bored silly at the same time? — Can you be happy if you are deprived of or unable to have sex? — Can you be happy without a belief in an afterlife? — Can you be happy while in poor health or chronic pain? — Can you be happy living paycheck to paycheck? — Do you think you're happier than most people, less happy than most, or about average? — Do some people seem to be trying too hard to be happy, to get attention, to upstage others?)

544. **HAPPINESS: Happiness is the absence of pain.** ....
....T-F / NI-PC-DB
➤ (Are you happy in homeostasis? — Is homeostasis boring? — Is stability an essential component of happiness?)

545. **HAPPINESS: People are always trying their best, within their level of awareness, to be happy, happier, or less unhappy.** ....T-F / NI-PC-DB
➤ (Is this premise contradicted by suicide & health-defeating behavior? — Can suicide be sane? —)

— Philosophy —

546. **HAPPINESS: People need much less to be happy than they think they do.**......................................T-F / NI-PC-DB

547. **HAPPINESS: Which would you rather be, if you couldn't be both? — <u>A</u>. happy, <u>B</u>. rich ..... A-B / NI-PC-DB**

548. **HONESTY: Honesty is the best policy — <u>A</u>. always, <u>B</u>. usually, <u>C</u>. sometimes, <u>D</u>. rarely.** ....A-B-C-D / NI-PC-DB
    ➤ (Are you willing to share things about yourself that one might consider against your self-interest? — Does it ever pay to <u>not</u> know the truth about an intimate's feelings, opinions, or history? — How long can a relationship last if it's under a permanent cloud of suspicion & distrust? — Do you prefer the truth even if it hurts?)

549. **INDISPENSABLE: No one is indispensable, everyone is expendable.** ....T-F / NI-PC-DB
    ➤ (Does limiting your answer to a work environment change your answer?)

550. **JUSTIFICATION: The ends justify the means. — <u>A</u>. always, <u>B</u>. usually, <u>C</u>. sometimes, <u>D</u>. rarely.** ....
    ....A-B-C-D / NI-PC-DB
    ➤ (Is this statement overused to justify or rationalize illegal, immoral or unethical means?)

551. **KNOW THYSELF: Is the ancient philosophical Greek philosophy of 'Know Thyself,' advocated by Socrates, Plato & Aristotle, still worth pursing today?** ....Y-N / NI-PC-DB

552. **LIES: Everyone lies.** ....T-F / NI-PC-DB
    ➤ (When is lying acceptable or justified? — How truthful is 'truth in advertising,' or truth in politics? — How do you respond or relate to deceit, dishonesty & hypocrisy? — Is it human nature to rationalize, justify, excuse or lie to defend against character attacks directed at yourself or family?)

— Philosophy —

553. **LIFE: In one word, complete this sentence, life is blank:** ....**NI-PC-DB**
➤ (e.g, — priceless — unfair — a game — a struggle — a battle — a bitch — a challenge — a story — a journey — a marathon — exciting — interesting — an adventure — a test — other)

554. **LIFE: Life is not fair**.....................................**T-F / NI-PC-DB**

555. **LIFE APPROACH: Which approach to life do you prefer — A. everything in moderation, B. all in, damn the consequences, C. nothing in excess?** ....
....**A-B C / NI-PC-DB**
➤ (How do the words 'the razor's edge' & balance fit into you life philosophy?)

556. **LIFE APPROACH: Which is more important to you — A. the destination, reaching goals, B. the journey, the pursuit?**..**A-B / NI-PC-DB**
➤ (Do you feel successful only when you achieve your goals or whenever you're making progress?)

557. **LIFE APPROACH: Which advice do you prefer, live everyday as if it were — A. your last, B. a second chance, C. the very first day of the rest of your life, D. the most important day of the present, without comparison?**..**A-B-C-D / NI-PC-DB**

558. **LIFE APPROACH: Do you prefer to live a life of — A. simplicity, minimalism & keeping a small footprint, B. a life focused on conspicuous consumption & living large?**
....**A-B / NI-PC-DB**

559. **LIFE INFLUENCE: How much of an influence do 'self-talk' & 'self-fulfilling prophecies' have on behavior, feelings & life experience? — A. major, B. minor** ....
....**A-B / NI-PC-DB**

— Philosophy —

560. **LIFE INFLUENCE: Our 'health & physical being' are mostly the result of** — **A.** genetics & nature, **B.** nurture, love, environment & experience, **C.** free will, choice & personal responsibility, **D.** determinism & fate, **E.** diet, exercise & good habits? ....**A-B-C-D-E / NI-PC-DB**

561. **LIFE INFLUENCE: Our 'mental & emotional lives' are mostly the result of** — **A.** genetics & nature, **B.** nurture love, environment & experience, **C.** free will, choice & personal responsibility, **D.** determinism & fate, **E.** diet, exercise & good habits? ....**A-B-C-D-E / NI-PC-DB**

562. **LIFESTYLE: Do you prefer a lifestyle of** — **A.** change, challenge & variety, **B.** routine, predictability & familiarity? ....**A-B / NI-PC-DB**

563. **MEANING & PURPOSE: Do you have a guiding meaning & purpose?** ....**Y-N / NI-PC-DB**
➤ (How important is it to have one? — Has it changed over time? — Does having 'meaning & purpose' affect your excitement about life?)

564. **MIND: Since life is a 'head-trip,' our highest priority should be the development of our minds.**....................
....**T-F / NI-PC-DB**
➤ (How do you develop your mind?)

565. **MIND: The mind can't tell the difference between that which is real & that which is vividly imagined.** ....
....**T-F / NI-PC-DB**
➤ (If true, does this support the premise that 'perception is reality,) until proven otherwise'? — Which is more important, what you think is or what is?)

— Philosophy —

566. MOTIVATION: No one does anything for nothing. ....
....T-F / NI-PC-DB
➤ (Which is a stronger motivator, **e.g.,** love — hate — fear — anger — recognition — money — desire — wants — needs — have-tos — desire to belong — desire to be true to one's identity — one's meaning & purpose? — Do you like revenge movies?)

567. NEVER: Never say never. ....T-F / NI-PC-DB

568. PEOPLE: The best way to handle people is tell them what they want to hear. ....T-F / NI-PC-DB

569. PEOPLE: People are basically selfish. ....T-F / NI-PC-DB
➤ (Is selfless the opposite of selfish? —Is altruistic behavior that makes you feel good truly self-less, since it personally benefits you emotionally?)

570. PEOPLE: People are basically good. ....T-F / NI-PC-DB

571. PEOPLE: People want & seek attention & will do almost anything to avoid being ignored. ....
....T-F / NI-PC-DB
➤ (Is it true that negative strokes or critical feedback is better than no attention at all? — What's the craziest or dumbest thing you've ever done to get attention or noticed?)

572. PEOPLE: Most people believe it's better to give than receive. ....T-F / NI-PC-DB

573. PEOPLE: Most people prefer acceptance & approval over constructive criticism. ....T-F / NI-PC-DB
➤ (If true, would it be helpful to 'sandwich each slice of criticism between two slices of praise'?)

574. PHILOSOPHY: Every life philosophy is debatable. ....
....T-F / NI-PC-DB
➤ (Can you name one that's not?)

— Philosophy —

575. **RESULTS: Everything happens for the best.** ....
....**T-F / NI-PC-DB**
➤ (According to whom? — Would this include getting maimed in an auto accident, or losing a loved one to a horrible disease?)

576. **RULES: All rules have their exceptions.** .....**T-F / NI-PC-DB**
➤ (Are there exceptions to the rule of 'no torture.'? — Are your rules rigid or flexible?)

577. **SALES: Everyone's in sales.** ....**T-F / NI-PC-DB**
➤ (Does this apply only to selling products in exchange for money, or does it include selling one's...**e.g.,** services — ideas & opinions — efforts — knowledge — time & labor? — How about persuading someone to comply with a request? — Do children sell? — What qualities make someone a 'good salesperson'?)

578. **SECRETS: Everyone has their secrets.** ......**T-F / NI-PC-DB**
➤ (Is there truth to the idea, 'we're only as sick as our secrets'?

579. **SQUEAKY WHEEL: Is your behavior ever influenced by the phrase, 'the squeaky wheel gets the grease'? .**
....**Y-N / NI-PC-DB**

580. **STRESS: Stress & happiness are mainly a function of — A. attitude, B. external conditions & circumstances, C. choices, D. time constraints, E. the unknown, F. matching expectations with reality?** .**A-B-C D-E-F / NI-PC-DB**
➤ (causes, **e.g.,** traffic — technology problems — deadlines & time limits — remodeling your home — moving to a new home in a new city — living with threats & ultimatums — unrealistic goals & expectations — impossible demands — waiting on the outcome of a critical health concern — major undesired changes or disruptions in plans or lifestyle — sudden changes in the dynamics of your interpersonal relationships — financial problems — medical problems including those of a loved one — caregiving — too many unresolved issues at one time — non-productive, unabating guilt or regret — pain — other / When the phone rings, do you assume it's good news, bad news, a robocall, a wrong number, a friendly 'just-to-say hello' call, or nothing important?)

— Philosophy —

581. **STRESS: How can & how do people handle stress?** ....
....**NI-PC-DB**
➤ (they eat — drink — do drugs — smoke — take hot tub or warm
baths — listen to music — exercise — hang on an inversion
machine — spend time in a sensory deprivation tank — confront the
source — have sex — get a massage — meditate — walk —
practice deep breathing — go to sleep — focus on blessings —
seek counseling — talk to close friends — read or listen to positive
materials — turn to their faith — change deadlines — reorder
priorities — get organized — drop low-payoff activities — eliminate
non-critical obligations — learn how to say no — pray, especially the
Serenity Prayer — change one's attitude or perspective — other —
To what degree does stress affect blood pressure?)

582. **SUCCESS: Besides talent, which factor is** most
important to becoming successful — **A.** attitude &
personality, **B.** intelligence, **C.** hard work & persistence,
D. connections & relationships, **E.** desire **F.** luck, timing
& chance. ....**A-B-C-D-E-F / NI-PC-DB**
➤ (In three short phrases what advice would you give your children
to help them live happy, successful lives, **e.g.,** Always do what's
right. — Stay humble. — Love your work. — Stay positive?)

583. **SUCCESS & HAPPINESS: A successful & happy life**
depends on — **A.** getting there, meaning achieving
major goals, **B.** learning to enjoy the journey, **C.** having
goals worthy of pursuit ....**A-B-C / NI-PC-DB**
➤ (Are your current feelings of success & happiness based more on
the past, recent experience, or what's happening presently?)

— Philosophy —

584. **TRAGEDY: What category does the worse day of your life fall into?**— **A.** work. job, or money. **B.** self-respect or mental health, **C.** loss or death of a loved one, **D.** rejection or betrayal by a partner or love interest, **E.** criticism of your smarts or intelligence, **F.** legal issues, **G.** attacks on your character, **H.** meaning & purpose, **I.** physical body or illness, **J.** Other? ....
...................................**A-B-C-D-E-F-G-H-I-J / NI-PC-DB**
➤ (How many 'worse days of your life' have you experienced?)

585. **TRUTH: Which is true most often** — **A.** the truth will set you free. **B.** the truth hurts, **C.** most people can't handle the truth? ....**A-B-C / NI-PC-DB**
➤ (On balance, is facing, admitting & sharing an uncomfortable truth about yourself preferable to hiding it, avoiding it or repressing it? — How are facts & truth the same; how & when are they different?)

586. **UNIQUENESS: Do you believe that although everyone is unique, not everyone truly feels unique?** ....
....**Y-N / NI-PC-DB**
➤ (Do you see a correlation between uniqueness & incompatibility? — How unique are you? — Do you ever compare yourself, your clothes, intelligence, or wealth to others? — Does comparing yourself to others make you feel superior, better than, or inferior, less than? — Do you buy the premise that you are a monopoly in time & place?)

587. **WORDS: Relative to your life, what are the 5 most important individual words in the English language?**
....**NI-PC-DB**
➤ (**e.g.,** fun — health — money — freedom — love — What are the odds of picking the same 5 words as someone else?)

— Philosophy —

588. **WORDS: Words count, words matter, words have consequences, but actions matter more.** ....
....T-F / NI-PC-DB
➤ (Can words comfort & heal ? — How much pain can words cause? — Can painful words be erased with loving actions?)

589. **WORRY: Are successful people who are problem-free & happy in all areas of life 'worry-free'?**
....Y-N / NI-PC-DB
➤ (Does everyone have fears, doubts, worries & insecurities? — How comfortable are you in sharing yours?)

18. **POLITICS & GOVERNMENT**

Important! Please read.

TABLE OF CONTENTS — Page 5
23 Chapters Listed Alphabetically — 723 Main Questions —
Key words in each chapter are in alphabetical order for that chapter.

ANSWER CHOICES
Y-N (Yes No) — T-F (True False) — A-B-C (Multiple Choice)
NI (Non-Issue) — PC (Potential Conflict) — DB (Deal Breaker)

HOW TO ADDRESS THE QUESTIONS
Whether you're in a relationship or not, answer first for yourself, then ask yourself, how would you feel if your partner or a potential partner were to choose differently or the opposite? If reviewing with a partner and areas of disagreement arise, engage your sense of humor, remain calm, and discuss your differences civilly.

JUDGING AN ENTRY
Whatever you feel about an entry, be careful not to underestimate the value of what may appear to be a petty or trivial issue. You'd be surprised, or maybe not, at how little it can take to start an argument or reveal a major difference of opinion. A discussion of these minor issues can sometimes be quite revelatory..

RIGHT & WRONG
There are no absolutely right or wrong answers, just your subjective opinions expressed as a starting point for deliberation or discussion.

— *Politics* —

590. **ABUSE: Which branch do you think is most susceptible to abuse of power?** — **A**. the legislative, **B**. the judicial, **C**. the executive? ....**A-B-C / NI-PC-DB**
➤ (Are you concerned about abuse of power by elected officials?)

591. **ECONOMICS: Do you understand economic terms?**
....**Y-N / NI-PC-DB**
➤ (recession — inflation — employment rates — fed rates — value of the dollar)

592. **ELECTION: Do you believe that Russia affected the outcome of our 2016 election?** ....**Y-N / NI-PC-DB**
Do you believe our elections are generally fair?

593. **FREEDOM: Which is more important** — **A**. freedom, **B**. security? ....**A-B / NI-PC-DB**

594. **FREEDOM: Which is more important** — **A**. freedom of religion, **B**. freedom of speech? ....**A-B / NI-PC-DB**
➤ (Is free-speech protection for parody & satire too liberal or too restrictive? — freedom of vs. freedom from religion)

595. **INFORMATION: What are you regular sources of political information?** ....**NI-PC-DB**
➤ (Can you distinguish between news & editorials? — How do you separate lies from the truth? — Do you listen to sources that promote positions that are contrary to yours?)

596. **INTEREST: Are you** — **A**. actively involved in politics, **B**. follow political news, **C**. have little interest in politics? ......
....**A-B-C / NI-PC-DB**
➤ (How familiar are you with The Pentagon Papers — Watergate — the Russia Probe — impeachment? — Are the concepts of corruption & draining the swamp of concern to you? — Are you for or against leaks from the White House? — How important is the rule of law? — Is the threat of impeachment necessary & sufficient to keep a president from abusing his or her power? — Are you for or against term-limits? — Are you for or against the "filibuster"?)

— Politics —

597. **INVESTIGATION: If you were on a political intelligence oversight committee, which of the following would influence your judgment the most?** — **A.** loyalty & allegiance to your party, **B.** the character of the individual being investigated, **C.** the effect your decision would have on your political power & ambitions, **D.** the law, **E.** your personal judgment of right & wrong, **F.** input from your family & friends, **G.** your religion, **H.** newscasts, **I.** patriotism, **J.** ego, K. how the country would be effected ....**A-B-C-D-E-F-G-H-I-J-K / NI-PC-DB**
➤ (Do the terms 'deep state,' 'cabal', 'QAnon' disturb you? — Are you familiar with The Pentagon Papers — Watergate — the Russia Probe? — Are the concepts of waste, abuse, fraud, corruption & draining the swamp of concern to you? — Are you for or against leaks from the White House?)

598. **LOCAL: "All politics is local."**.....................**T-F / NI-PC-DB**

599. **MATE: Is it important for your mate or partner to share your political ideology?**............................**Y-N / NI-PC-DB**

600. **MOTIVATION: Do most politicians become politicians** — **A.** to serve their constituents, **B.** to serve themselves & their family, **C.** to serve their tribe, faction, or party, **D.** to defend & support the constitution & the law?
....**A-B-C-D / NI-PC-DB**
➤ (Do you believe most politicians want to be feared without being hated or disliked?)

— Politics —

601. **NATIONAL SECURITY: What's your attitude toward national security?** ....NI-PC-DB

➤ (defense budget — size & strength of the military — weapons of mass destruction **re:** used, given away, stolen, sold, destroyed — treaties — international terrorism — domestic terrorism — Homeland Security — NSC — CIA — NSA — FBI — illegal & legal immigration — border security — travel bans — arms & drug trade — sanctions — protection of our electoral process — Patriot Act — security clearances — United Nations — allies — enemies — national emergency act)

602. **PARTY IDENTIFICATION: How do you identify yourself politically?** ....NI-PC-DB

➤ (Democrat — Republican — Tea party — Freedom Caucus — independent — unregistered — progressive — radical — communist — socialist — capitalist — benevolent capitalist — Green Party — Libertarian — nationalist — globalist — economic nationalist — democratic socialist — white nationalist — alt-right — globalist — populist — patriot — isolationist — internationalist — interventionist — protectionist — conservative — liberal — centrist — moderate — financially conservative & socially liberal — democratic socialist — right-wing — left-wing — other — Can a relationship survive if the partners have strong, diverse political ideologies? — Are you for or against including a 'Citizenship' question on the 2020 census forms? — Is identity politics (religion, race, ethnicity, social, cultural) divisive or an example of our diversity?)

603. **POLITICAL JOB: If you could wave a magic wand, which of the following government positions would you like?** ....A-B-C-D-E-F-G / NI-PC-DB

— **A.** cabinet position of your choice, **B.** president, **C.** vice president, **D.** secretary of state, **E.** national security advisor, **F.** chief of staff, **G.** gate-keeper to the president's office

— Politics —

604. PROMISES: Which of the following promises do you most want to hear from a politician? ....NI-PC-DB

➤ (they will, **e.g.,** add jobs — unify the country — improve our standing in the world — stamp out corruption — avoid conflict of interests — lower taxes — raise minimum wage — improve the economy — guarantee universal basic income — protect social security — pass the ERA amendment — support reparations — improve health care **re:** single payer — public option — universal coverage — make America safer — stricter gun laws — secure our borders — support law & order — balance the budget — reduce the deficit — avoid war — win war if in process — promote religious freedom — reform immigration laws — reform the IRS — reform voting laws — fix infrastructure — inspire us to greater achievement — reform election laws — support the Me Too Movement — protect our environment — make us proud to be Americans)

605. TAXES & BUDGET: What's your attitude toward taxes & the federal budget? ....NI-PC-DB

➤ (taxes **i.e.,** income — luxury — estate — self-employment — business — corporate — capital gains — sales/consumption — tax rates, **i.e.,** flat tax — progressive — regressive — or proportional — tax reform & its effect on the poor, middle class & wealthy — investment in infrastructure & heath-care — balanced budget — free trade — trade wars — tariffs — deficit spending —earmarks & pork spending — debt ceiling — social security — entitlements — taxes paid in — governmental safety net & welfare — government shutdowns — national emergencies)

606. VOTING: What's your attitude toward voting? ....
....NI-PC-DB

➤ (city, state, federal — why you vote — why you don't — source of decision making knowledge & information — Is voting a duty? — How do you feel about gerrymandering & redistricting? — If you don't vote, do you have a right to complain about the job government is doing? — Do you prefer the electoral college or popular vote in presidential elections? — Which is more important, likability or electability?)

— Politics —

607. **WAR & MILITARY: What's your attitude toward war & the military industrial complex?** ....NI-PC-DB

➤ (budget — refugees — women in combat — transgenders in military — international human rights — despotic governments — preemptive strikes — morality of torture & enhanced interrogation techniques — dove or hawk — drone strikes — weapon autonomy — regime change — allies — NATO — boots on the ground — arming & training of foreign forces — direct talks with military adversaries or enemies — conventional war — nuclear war — dirty bombs — intercontinental ballistic missiles — cyber warfare — treaties & alliances)

19. <u>RELATIONSHIPS</u>

<u>*Important! Please read.*</u>

<u>TABLE OF CONTENTS</u> — Page 5

23 Chapters Listed Alphabetically — 723 Main Questions —

Key words in each chapter are in alphabetical order for that chapter.

<u>ANSWER CHOICES</u>

Y-N (Yes No) — T-F (True False) — A-B-C (Multiple Choice)

NI (Non-Issue) — PC (Potential Conflict) — DB (Deal Breaker)

<u>HOW TO ADDRESS THE QUESTIONS</u>

Whether you're in a relationship or not, answer first for yourself, then ask yourself, how would you feel if your partner or a potential partner were to choose differently or the opposite? If reviewing with a partner and areas of disagreement arise, engage your sense of humor, remain calm, and discuss your differences civilly.

<u>JUDGING AN ENTRY</u>

Whatever you feel about an entry, be careful not to underestimate the value of what may appear to be a petty or trivial issue. You'd be surprised, or maybe not, at how little it can take to start an argument or reveal a major difference of opinion. A discussion of these minor issues can sometimes be quite revelatory..

<u>RIGHT & WRONG</u>

There are no absolutely right or wrong answers, just your subjective opinions expressed as a starting point for deliberation or discussion.

☆☆☆☆☆

— Relationships —

608. **ALONENESS: What's the difference between loneliness & aloneness?** ....NI-PC-DB

609. **ANNOYING: Does the statement 'people can be so annoying' also apply to you?**...................Y-N / NI-PC-DB
➤ (Do you have a partner or friends who get on your nerves? — What's most annoying about your partner or best friend?)

610. **BELIEF: How would you handle knowing that you saw or heard something consequential, but no one believed you & you couldn't prove it?** ....NI-PC-DB

611. **BREAKING UP: Do most relationships break up over — A. big things, B. cumulative small things?**...................
....A-B / NI-PC-DB

612. **BREAKING UP: How do people break up?** ....NI-PC-DB
➤ (in person — email — letter — phone — through a friend — ignore & avoid — text — tweet — other — What's the preferred way? — Does 'it's me not you' help the dumpee? — Have you ever had a relationship end suddenly, with no explanation & no understanding of why?)

613. **CONCEPTS: What's your attitude toward these relationship concepts?** ....NI-PC-DB
➤ (commitment — intimacy — loyalty — fidelity — monogamy & exclusivity — security & predictability — pillow talk, puffery & promises)

614. **CONFESSION: Confession is good for the soul — A. always, B. usually, C. sometimes, D. rarely.** ....
....A-B-C-D / NI-PC-DB
➤ (What are the pluses & minuses of confession? — Does it depend on to whom you're confessing & the subject matter of the confession?)

— Relationships —

615. **COUPLES: Every couple goes through their ups & downs.** ....T-F / NI-PC-DB
➤ (Why do you think partners are willing to stay in relationships built on more downs than ups?)

616. **DISAPPOINTMENTS: Has anyone important to you ever painfully disappointed you?** ....Y-N / NI-PC-DB
➤ (your child — a spouse — a best friend — a boss — a parent — a lover)

617. **ENDED: How far would you go to learn why a relationship ended, abruptly, without explanation?**
— **A.** very far, **B.** somewhat far, **C.** not far at all...............
....A-B-C / NI-PC-DB
➤ (Would your reaction be different if the relationship involved a friend, a business connection, an acquaintance, or a love interest?)

618. **EXES: Is the quality of your partner's relationship with their ex important to you?** — **A.** very, **B.** moderately, **C.** somewhat, **D.** not at all ....A-B-C-D / NI-PC-DB

619. **EXES: How would you be affected by your partner's prominent display of their ex's pictures, memorabilia, or an urn?** — **A.** very, **B.** moderately, **C.** somewhat, **D.** not at all..........................A-B-C-D / NI-PC-DB

620. **FAMILY: Is the acceptance & approval of your relationship(s) by your parents &/or friends important to you?** — **A.** very, **B.** moderately, **C.** somewhat, **D.** not at all..........................A-B-C-D / NI-PC-DB
➤ (Are any of your friends or family members upset with you at the present time? — At family events, are you relaxed & spontaneous, or do you often feel inclined to hold your tongue & choose your words very carefully? — How important to you is your inner-circle?)

— Relationships —

621. **FAMILY: How are your relationships with your parents — siblings — in-laws — emergency contacts?** ....
....**NI-PC-DB**
➤ (Do family members share dirty laundry or speak disparagingly of one another?—How do you feel about family reunions? — Do any of your relationships embarrass you?)

622. **FAMILY: Nothing is more important than family.** ....
....**T-F / NI-PC-DB**
➤ (Are you familiar with Dodie Smith's, "Dear Octopus?" — Do you hold your family & close friends to higher standards when it comes to living up to one's word?)

623. **FAMILY: Would you ever move away from your family to save a relationship?** ....**Y-N / NI-PC-DB**

624. **FRIENDS: Can you have more than one best friend?** ....
....**Y-N / NI-PC-DB**

625. **FRIENDS: What's your situation re: friends?** ....**NI-PC-DB**
➤ (close ones — old ones — new ones — mutual friends with your partner — work friends — friends of the opposite sex — family friends — Have you ever lost a friend without ever learning why? — How many real friends do you have? — Do you have any friends with whom you have nothing in common? — How many friends do you need on your side to not care about what others think about you or your opinions?)

— Relationships —

626. FRIENDS: How do you define a friend? ....NI-PC-DB
➤ (anyone you know who's not an enemy — anyone you refer to with the phrase, 'love ya' — anyone you enjoy talking to or visiting without an agenda — anyone who knows it's you & will take your call — anyone who helps you achieve your personal or professional goals or supports your efforts — anyone you can rant to who gives a damn — What distinguishes a friend from an acquaintance? — Are all associates considered friends? — How many of your Facebook friends are 'true' friends? — Does the label of 'friend' suggest a degree of trust & loyalty? — How many of your friends or family do you talk to on a regular basis, at least weekly? — What determines when a friendly acquaintance can be introduced as a friend? — Do you have any enemies? — What qualities does one exhibit that justify being called a friend? — What behavior or personality characteristics justify ending a friendship?)

627. FRIENDS: What topics do you generally talk about with your friends? ....NI-PC-DB
➤ (TV — movies — entertainment — famous people/celebrities — politics — health — food — technology — sports — hot news topics — maintenance of car & home — relationships — spirituality — God or religion — gossip — weather — travel — sex — business — investments — purchases — bargains — how to save or make money — other — Do you have different friends for different topics?)

628. FRIENDSHIP: Would you maintain a friendship with someone you considered judgmental, critical & unforgiving; someone who regularly reminded you of your shortcomings, flaws & past mistakes, including incidents where you exhibited poor judgment?..Y-N / NI-PC-DB
➤ (Do you have friends you consider petty, picky, weird, or flakey?)

629. FULFILLMENT: Do you have people in your life who make your life more fulfilling because they care about you & believe in you & your dreams ....
....Y-N / NI-PC-DB

— Relationships —

630. **HATE: Are any of your friendships based on common hates, or on the idea that 'the enemy of my enemy is my friend'?**...Y-N / NI-PC-DB

631. **HEALTHY: Is a healthy relationship, necessarily, the same as a compatible relationship?** ....Y-N / NI-PC-DB

632. **HOME: What does the phrase, 'you can't go home again' mean?**...NI-PC-DB

633. **IMPORTANCE: Relationships are everything.**.................
....T-F / NI-PC-DB

634. **INTRODUCTIONS: Do you believe in the idea that each person on the planet is only six introductions away from contacting any other person on the planet?** ....
....Y-N / NI-PC-DB
➤ (How can this '6-degrees of separation' principle manifest in selling efforts, business promotions, background investigations or seeking medical help?)

635. **LOYALTY: How important is loyalty in your relationships? — A.** extremely, **B.** very, **C.** moderately ..
....A-B-C / NI-PC-DB
➤ (How far does loyalty go? — sticking up for someone when they've screwed up — keeping their lies a secret — willingness to break the law to protect them — defending their reputation — characterizing their mistakes with a positive spin — assume the best of their motives & reasons — living up to non-disclosure agreements — not selling someone out to cover your own ass — etc. — Is loyalty to a spouse, boss, or business parter greater or the same as loyalty to a family member or friend? — Does loyalty imply allegiance, obedience & devotion? — How do you handle divided loyalties? — Who's more loyal, men or women?)

636. **MONEY: Statistically, which relationship is more likely to fail? — A.** one in which money is no object **B.** one in which money is very much an object...........A-B / NI-PC-DB

— Relationships —

637. **OPPOSITES: Opposites attract.** ....T-F / NI-PC-DB
➤ (introvert-extrovert — good girl-bad boy & vice versa — worldly-unworldly — wealthy-poor — college educated-high school only — extremely attractive-average — Can opposites be complementary?)

638. **OTHERS' OPINIONS: What do you think of people who say, "I don't give a damn what anyone thinks of me"? —** **A.** they're strong, independent & confident, **B.** it's a defense mechanism, **C.** they're jerks, **D.** as a social being we all care about what some people think of us .....
....A-B-C-D / NI-PC-DB

639. **PARTNERSHIP: Do you consider yourself —** **A.** a partnership person, **B.** independent, prefer to live alone?
....A-B / NI-PC-DB

640. **PREVIOUS: How willing are you to discuss your previous close relationships?**..........................NI-PC-DB
➤ (loves — live-ins — marriage(s) — engagement(s) — platonic friends — friends with benefits — other)

641. **PRIVACY: Do intrusive relatives & family members create privacy problems?** ....Y-N / NI-PC-DB

642. **RELATIONSHIPS: Is the following quote, "Almost all of our relationships begin, and most of them continue, as forms of mutual exploitation, i.e., a mental or physical barter, to be terminated when one or both parties run out of goods"? —** **A.** basically true, **B.** cynical? ....A-B / NI-PC-DB
➤ (How long can a one-sided relationship, one that is not mutually rewarding or emotionally satisfying, be expected to last?)

— Relationships —

643. **SECRETS & LIES: What's your attitude toward secrets & lies?**...**NI-PC-DB**
➤ (cheating & betrayal — lies **re:** criminal & health history — well-intentioned lies — lies to protect another's feelings — white lies — courtesy lies— gross exaggerations — unforgivable lies — lies under oath — plausible deniability — rolling disclosure — lies of omission, **e.g.,** jail time — an ex — a child — or — a bankruptcy — effect on trust if the lies or secrets are uncovered — What does playing it close to the vest imply? — What does the phrase 'I'll never lie to you' mean? — Are secrets lies by omission? — Does everyone lie? — How would you respond to the knowledge that someone you trusted revealed a secret of yours?)

644. **SPECIAL DAYS: What are your expectations re: special days?**...**NI-PC-DB**
➤ (Anniversaries — Birthdays — Valentine's Day — Easter — Thanksgiving — Christmas — Mother's Day — Father's Day — dinner — gifts — cards — trips — party)

645. **TIME:** (see **Time** main heading) ....**NI-PC-DB**

646. **TRUST: How is trust in a relationship established? — A.** earned or built over time, **B.** blindly accepted out the gate & continued till broken based on betrayal or lies, **C.** established based on promises expressed with reassuring words ....**A-B-C / NI-PC-DB**
➤ (How important is consistency in establishing & maintaining trust? — How many lies or broken promises does it take to permanently destroy trust? — Does your answer depend on the size of the lies or importance of the promises? — Does the word 'promise' mean try, best intentions, or guarantee? — Does not returning a promised phone call constitute a small breach of trust?)

— Relationships —

647. **TRUST: Who besides your partner do you trust with keys to your home, safe deposit box, bank accounts, or passwords to your cell phone or computer?** ....
....**NI-PC-DB**
➤ (How many people would you trust with your life, your car? — How many people do you know that you consider very reliable, dependable & trustworthy? — Do you share cellphone passwords with anyone?)

648. **UNCONVENTIONAL: How do you view relationships involving significant age differences between a man & a woman?** ....**NI-PC-DB**
➤ (Does the size of the age difference affect your view? — older woman & younger man — younger woman & older man — Do the words cougar, gold-digger, sugar daddy, or cradle robber come to mind? — Besides age, what makes for a complicated relationship?

649. **WHY: Is it human nature to not like unanswered questions, especially those related to intriguing emotional mysteries, riddled with questions that begin with 'Why'?** ....**Y-N / NI-PC-DB**

650. **WINNING: Which is more important to you — A. winning an argument & proving you're right, B. peace & the health of the relationship?** ....**A-B / NI-PC-DB**
➤ (What arguments are you having that are not open to further debate, **e.g.,** driving under the influence — moving out of the area — having or not having kids — quitting a job — buying a new car — other?)

See also Dating, Live-in, Love, Marriage & Sex main headings.

20. **RELIGION**

Important! Please read.

TABLE OF CONTENTS — Page 5

23 Chapters Listed Alphabetically — 723 Main Questions —

Key words in each chapter are in alphabetical order for that chapter.

ANSWER CHOICES

Y-N (Yes No) — T-F (True False) — A-B-C (Multiple Choice)

NI (Non-Issue) — PC (Potential Conflict) — DB (Deal Breaker)

HOW TO ADDRESS THE QUESTIONS

Whether you're in a relationship or not, answer first for yourself, then ask yourself, how would you feel if your partner or a potential partner were to choose differently or the opposite? If reviewing with a partner and areas of disagreement arise, engage your sense of humor, remain calm, and discuss your differences civilly.

JUDGING AN ENTRY

Whatever you feel about an entry, be careful not to underestimate the value of what may appear to be a petty or trivial issue. You'd be surprised, or maybe not, at how little it can take to start an argument or reveal a major difference of opinion. A discussion of these minor issues can sometimes be quite revelatory..

RIGHT & WRONG

There are no absolutely right or wrong answers, just your subjective opinions expressed as a starting point for deliberation or discussion.

☆☆☆☆☆

— *Religion* —

651. **APOCALYPSE: Do you believe in the apocalypse or armageddon?** ....Y-N / NI-PC-DB

652. **BELIEFS: Do you believe in any of the following?** ....
....Y-N / NI-PC-DB
➤ (salvation — prayer — miracles — rapture — eternal life — karma — reincarnation — angels — redemption)

653. **CHEMICAL: There are no chemical solutions to spiritual problems.** ....T-F / NI-PC-DB

654. **FOUNDATION: What is your religious or spiritual foundation?**...NI-PC-DB
➤ (Buddhism — Catholicism — Christianity — Church of Religious Science — Confucianism — Hinduism — Islamism — Jehovah's Witness — Judaism — Zionism — Mormonism — Protestantism — Scientology — 7th Day Adventists — Shintoism — Taoism — Unitarianism — Wiccan — atheism — agnosticism — deism — evangelicalism — ethical humanism — theism — Zoroastrianism — Marxism — born-again — Jew for Jesus — other — Are you religiously tolerant? — How do you explain the large number of religious denominations? — Why do bad things happen to good people or innocent children? — Are 'workism' & environmentalism new religions? — In a plane crash does God play a role in who lives & who dies?)

655. **GOD: Do you believe in God, a higher power, or some form of supreme being?** ....Y-N / NI-PC-DB
➤ (Can an atheist or agnostic live a moral life? — Can you believe in God without being religious? — How many Gods are there? — What's the difference between a belief in God & faith that God exists? — In a word, what is God, a concept, a being, a metaphysical reality, the creator of the universe, other? — Do you believe Jesus is God, the son of God, a man, or a combination?)

656. **GOD: Is being a critical thinker, a believer in science & cause & effect incompatible with a belief in a just & loving God?** ....Y-N / NI-PC-DB

— Religion —

657. **GOLDEN RULE: Do you live by the golden rule?** ....
....**Y-N / NI-PC-DB**
➤ (Is it okay to do a bad, wrong or illegal thing for the right reason, a righteous cause, or a greater good? — When violating the law, for whatever your reason, should you expect to suffer the legal consequences?)

658. **HEAVEN: Do you believe in heaven & hell?** ....
....**Y-N / NI-PC-DB**
➤ (Do people experience heaven & hell on earth?)

659. **MATE: Is it important for your mate or partner to share your religious-belief system?** ....**Y-N / NI-PC-DB**
➤ (Would you convert to your partner's religion to save your relationship?)

660. **ORIGIN: Do you believe in — A.** evolution, **B.** punctuated equilibrium, **C.** the literal bible account of creation, **D.** the Big Bang theory, **E.** Combination? ....
....**A-B-C-D-E / NI-PC-DB**
➤ (Are the words mutation, natural selection, & evolution related?)

661. **RELIGION: Religion can answer most or all of our problems.** ....**T-F / NI-PC-DB**

662. **RELIGION: Religion causes many of our relationship problems.** ....**T-F / NI-PC-DB**

663. **RELIGION: To what degree are you involved in, knowledgable of, or committed to your religion? — A.** very, **B.** moderately, **C.** somewhat, **D.** not at all ....
....**A-B-C-D / NI-PC-DB**

664. **SATAN: Do you believe in satan or the devil?** ....
....**Y-N / NI-PC-DB**

21. SEX

Important! Please read.

TABLE OF CONTENTS — Page 5

23 Chapters Listed Alphabetically — 723 Main Questions —

Key words in each chapter are in alphabetical order for that chapter.

ANSWER CHOICES

Y-N (Yes No) — T-F (True False) — A-B-C (Multiple Choice)

NI (Non-Issue) — PC (Potential Conflict) — DB (Deal Breaker)

HOW TO ADDRESS THE QUESTIONS

Whether you're in a relationship or not, answer first for yourself, then ask yourself, how would you feel if your partner or a potential partner were to choose differently or the opposite? If reviewing with a partner and areas of disagreement arise, engage your sense of humor, remain calm, and discuss your differences civilly.

JUDGING AN ENTRY

Whatever you feel about an entry, be careful not to underestimate the value of what may appear to be a petty or trivial issue. You'd be surprised, or maybe not, at how little it can take to start an argument or reveal a major difference of opinion. A discussion of these minor issues can sometimes be quite revelatory..

RIGHT & WRONG

There are no absolutely right or wrong answers, just your subjective opinions expressed as a starting point for deliberation or discussion.

☆☆☆☆☆

— Sex —

665. **BACHELOR PARTIES: How would you feel about your partner attending a bachelor or bachelorette party?** ..
....**NI-PC-DB**
➤ (Would it create any anxiety about fidelity?)

666. **CHEATING: If you learned that your partner occasionally had been seeing someone of the same or other sex for dinner, behind your back, but were told about the dinners & you believed there was no sexual intimacy, would you consider that cheating?**
....**NI-PC-DB**
➤ (What would you require of them before you could forgive their behavior for not telling you? — Is going to a strip club cheating? — Is fantasizing about someone other than your partner or looking but not touching forms of infidelity?)

667. **DISEASES: Do sexually transmitted diseases & infections concern you?** ....**Y-N / NI-PC-DB**
➤ (syphilis — gonorrhea — chlamydia — LGV — genital herpes — hepatitis — HPV — etc.)

668. **FLIRTING: What's your attitude toward flirting?** ....
....**NI-PC-DB**
➤ (being the recipient of it — you doing it — your partner doing it — Does or would your partner's flirting make you jealous, insecure, distrusting, or embarrassed?)

669. **FREQUENCY: How would you react to a measurable decline in the frequency of sex in your relationship?**
— **A.** broach the topic & openly discuss your feelings, **B.** begin to doubt whether you're loved or lovable, **C.** become sullen & passive-aggressive, **D.** bashfully hint & beat around the bush, **E.** consider using sex aids like porn or sex toys, **F.** assume the worst & have an affair ....
....**A-B-C-D-E / NI-PC-DB**

— Sex —

670. **HARASSMENT: How important an issue is sexual harassment?** — **A.** extremely, **B.** very, **C.** moderately, **D.** not very, **E.** unimportant ....**A-B-C-D-E / NI-PC-DB**
➤ (In addition to inappropriate sexual advances, sexual misconduct & indecent exposure, how affected are you when hearing about other sex crimes, **e.g.,** pedophilia — rape — sexual assault — incest — molestation or sexual abuse of a child or minor — sex slavery — prostitution? — How do you feel about workplace sexualized humor or sexual innuendo? — Issues, **i.e.,** power & privilege — force — consent — teasing — sex for favors — favors for sex — student-teacher encounters — punishment & consequences for crossing lines — Me Too, Time's Up & Never Again — Does no always mean no? — Are you as a consumer complicit if you watch, listen to, or purchase the products of an accused harasser? — sharing & reporting abuses — proving abuses)

671. **INFIDELITY: How many times would you forgive infidelity?** — **A.** once, **B.** more than once, **C.** zero ....
....**A-B-C / NI-PC-DB**

672. **INFIDELITY: Has porn or feminism had an effect on infidelity rates among men &/or women?**.....................
....**Y-N / NI-PC-DB**

673. **INFIDELITY: Is infidelity mainly a consequence of** — **A.** incompatibility, **B.** a lack of love, **C.** a lack of respect, **D.** boredom, **E.** unsatisfactory sex with partner, **F.** immature, impulsive behavior, **G.** payback, **H.**other? ....
....**A-B-C-D-E-F-G H / NI-PC-DB**

674. **INFIDELITY: Who is more likely to cheat?** — **A.** men, **B.** women ....**A-B / NI-PC-DB**

675. **INFIDELITY: Who is more likely to cheat?** — **A.** the rich &/or famous, **B.** the poor &/or middle class? ....
....**A-B / NI-PC-DB**

— Sex —

676. **JEALOUSY: How would you feel if your partner acted on an opportunity to meet up with an old flame?** ....
....NI-PC-DB
➤ (Would it make you feel insecure?)

677. **LOVEMAKING: How long do you think a lovemaking session should last, not including cuddling after?** .....
....NI-PC-DB

678. **MAKE-UP SEX: Can great 'makeup-sex' precipitate future fights?** ....Y-N / NI-PC-DB

679. **MARRIAGE: Do you believe in sex before marriage?** ....
....Y-N / NI-PC-DB
➤ (Do you believe that sex after marriage should always be as good & passionate as it was in the beginning? — Would you have sex with an ex after divorce?)

680. **NONE: How would you feel & what would you do if your partner became unable, because of a physical reason, to ever have sex again?** ....NI-PC-DB
➤ (Is impotence a deal breaker?)

681. **NUDITY What's your attitude toward you or a partner walking around the house nude?** ....NI-PC-DB
➤ (Is your answer the same if children are present? — Have you ever gone to a nudist resort; would you?)

682. **ONE-NIGHT STAND Would you ever engage in a one-night stand with the foreknowledge that that's what it was going to be?** ....Y-N / NI-PC-DB

— Sex —

683. **ORIENTATION: What's your sexual orientation &/or gender identity?** ....**NI-PC-DB**
➤ (LBGTQ — heterosexual — gay — homosexual — lesbian — bisexual — pansexual — non-monosexual — asexual — transexual — transgender — cisgender — non-binary — androgynous — gender fluid — hermaphrodite — beyond male & female — bicurious — polyamorous — swinger — committed — What's your attitude toward gender-labeling of bathrooms? — If gay, was coming out an issue? — What are your attitudes toward the LGBTQ community? — How would you respond to learning two years into your marriage that your spouse was gay or a cross-dresser?)

684. **PASSION: Which is more true?** — <u>**A.** sexual passion is evidence of great love, **B.** diminished sexual passion is a sign of waning love, **C.** neither</u> ....**A-B-C / NI-PC-DB**

685. **SEX: On a scale of 1 to 5, how important is sex in your life?** ....**1-2-3-4-5 / NI-PC-DB**

686. **SEX LIFE: Are you open to discussing your past sex life?**..**Y-N / NI-PC-DB**
➤ (virgin — promiscuous — Puritanical — unconventional — swinging — open relationships — long & short committed relationships —sexual abuse as a child)

687. **SEX LIFE: Do you or would you engage in any of the following sexual activities?** ....**Y-N / NI-PC-DB**
➤ (porn — threesomes — orgies — oral — anal— self or mutual masturbation — bondage & domination — sadomasochism — spanking — dangerous autoerotic asphyxiation — toe sucking —Do you or would you use: Viagra — vibrators — toys — whipped cream — hot dripping candle wax? — other)

— *Sex* —

688. **SEX LIFE: What are your sexual expectations in the bedroom?** ....**NI-PC-DB**
➤ (daily, weekly, monthly — long & slow sessions or quickies — routine or spontaneous — passionate or subdued — always consensual, never forced — hard & rough or soft & gentle — Are you hesitant to request something different for fear of rejection? — How would you handle erectile dysfunction in your partner? — Are there fetishes you won't tolerate? — How would unsatisfying sex affect your overall relationship?)

See also Dating, Live-in, Love, Marriage, Relationships, Communications main headings.

22. <u>SOCIAL ISSUES</u>

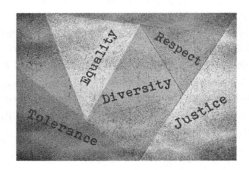

<u>Important! Please read.</u>

<u>TTABLE OF CONTENTS — Page 5</u>

23 Chapters Listed Alphabetically — 723 Main Questions —
Key words in each chapter are in alphabetical order for that chapter.

<u>ANSWER CHOICES</u>

Y-N (Yes No) — T-F (True False) — A-B-C (Multiple Choice)
NI (Non-Issue) — PC (Potential Conflict) — DB (Deal Breaker)

<u>HOW TO ADDRESS THE QUESTIONS</u>

Whether you're in a relationship or not, answer first for yourself, then ask yourself, how would you feel if your partner or a potential partner were to choose differently or the opposite? If reviewing with a partner and areas of disagreement arise, engage your sense of humor, remain calm, and discuss your differences civilly.

<u>JUDGING AN ENTRY</u>

Whatever you feel about an entry, be careful not to underestimate the value of what may appear to be a petty or trivial issue. You'd be surprised, or maybe not, at how little it can take to start an argument or reveal a major difference of opinion. A discussion of these minor issues can sometimes be quite revelatory..

<u>RIGHT & WRONG</u>

There are no absolutely right or wrong answers, just your subjective opinions expressed as a starting point for deliberation or discussion.

☆☆☆☆☆

— Social —

689. **ABORTION: Are you — A.** pro-life, **B.** pro-choice?............

....**A-B / NI-PC-DB**

➤ (Planned Parenthood — rape & incest? — When does life begin?)

690. **Ax Throwing: Are you familiar with the game of ax throwing**? ....**Y-N / NI-PC-DB**

➤ (Have you participated? — Would you play?)

691. **BULLYING: What's your attitude toward bullying in schools?** ....**NI-PC-DB**

➤ (cyber — emotional — physical — hazing — gossiping — trolling on social media — gangs — Should name-calling & labeling on school campuses be treated as a form of bullying?)

692. **CAPITAL PUNISHMENT: Are you — A.** for capital punishment, **B.** against it? ....**A-B / NI-PC-DB**

693. **DOMESTIC ABUSE: How important an issue is domestic abuse? — A.** extremely, **B.** very, **C.** moderately, **D.** not very, **E.** unimportant ....

....**A-B-C-D-E / NI-PC-DB**

➤ (How long would you stay in a relationship following a physical assault? — When does controlling behavior become abuse? — When does emotional, financial, or sexual abuse cross the 'red' line? — Do you agree that seeking help is a sign of strength, not weakness? — Is emotional blackmail a form of abuse? — In your opinion, are extreme outbursts of anger precursors to abuse? — Can you explain why someone might stay in an abusive relationship?)

694. **DRINKING: What's your attitude toward drinking** (See **Health, Fitness, Medical** main heading)......................**NI-PC-DB**

695. **DRUGS: What's your attitude toward drugs?** (see **Health, Fitness, Medical** main heading)......................**NI-PC-DB**

— Social —

696. **ENVIRONMENT: Are you concerned about the environment?** — **A.** very, **B.** somewhat, **C.** a little ....
....**A-B-C / NI-PC-DB**
➤ (global warming & climate change — living green — use of pesticides & chemical cleaning agents — waste disposal — recycling — composting — energy conservation — deforestation — solar — water, air, soil pollution — auto emission standards — fracking — strip-mining — wildlife habitat — EPA — Christmas trees real or artificial — Do you support banning polystyrene cups, plastic straws & plastic grocery bags? — Do you respect mother nature?)

697. **GAMBLING: What's your attitude toward gambling?**.....
....**NI-PC-DB**
➤ (casinos — poker with friends — online betting for sports or horse racing — Gamblers Anonymous — penalties — treatment)

698. **GOOD SAMARITAN LAW: What's your attitude toward good Samaritan laws?** ....**NI-PC-DB**
➤ (legal obligation to do the right thing **re:** helping someone in distress — protection from prosecution for a bad result while providing help)

699. **GUN CONTROL: What your attitude toward gun control?** ....**NI-PC-DB**
➤ (2nd amendment — ban & repeal — NRA — background checks — red flag laws — open carry — locked safes — age limits to buy or own — liability — gun shows — online gun auctions — ammunition sales — assault & automatic weapons — access & availability — stop, question & frisk — bump stocks — large magazines — use in a home break-in — self-defense — stand your ground — buy-back programs — rifles vs. handguns — concealed-carry reciprocity — armed teachers — student protests — USA laws vs other countries)

700. **HUMAN RIGHTS: How concerned are you about human rights?** — **A.** active advocate, **B.** concerned, **C.** little interest ....**A-B-C / NI-PC-DB**
➤ (in America — internationally — social justice vs. justice)

— Social —

701. **IMMIGRATION: How concerned are you about immigration?** — **A.** active advocate for or against, **B.** concerned, **C.** little interest ....A-B-C / NI-PC-DB
➤ (legal vs illegal immigration — undocumented — merit based — children of undocumented — chain immigration — criminals — refugees — productive vs. unproductive immigrants — length of time here — social cost — visa lotteries — green cards — tax contribution — voting rights — breakup of families — deportation — profiling — effect on jobs & wages — sanctuary cities & states — border control **re:** by agents, a wall, or technology — amnesty or path to citizenship — DACA, dreamers & Dream Act — jobs that many don't want — separation of undocumented families at border)

702. **LBGTQ COMMUNITY: What's your attitude toward gay rights & homosexuality?** ....NI-PC-DB
➤ (HIV — aids — gay marriage — legal & insurance issues — 'ask don't tell' — gay teachers — discrimination — Boy/Girl Scouts — military service-)

703. **POLICE: How concerned are you about police brutality or abuse of power?** — **A.** active advocate, **B.** concerned, **C.** little interest ....A-B-C / NI-PC-DB
➤ (statistics & facts — dash, gun & body cams — prejudice — riots — interracial shootings — white supremacy — penalties — teen involved shootings — support for law & order — violence — protests)

704. **PRISONS: What's your attitude toward prison reform?**
....NI-PC-DB
➤ (sentencing guidelines — incarceration & release policies — changing classification of crimes — recidivism — rehabilitation — vocational & educational training — punishment — retribution — overcrowding — cost per inmate per year — violent vs. non-violent crimes — victimless crimes — stand your ground laws — drug-related crimes — sexual crimes — murder — gang-related crimes — solitary confinement — guard training — restorative justice — mandatory minimums — humanizing vs. evil-criminal approach)

— Social —

705. PROSTITUTION: Are you — **A.** for the legalization of prostitution, **B.** against it? ....**A-B / NI-PC-DB**

706. RACISM: How big an issue is racism & bigotry in the U.S.A.? — **A.** very, **B.** growing, **C.** declining, **D.** small .....
....**A-B-C-D / NI-PC-DB**
➤ (Is your answer the same for worldwide?)

707. SELF-DRIVING CARS: How do you feel about self-driving cars, self-driving commercial trucks & pilotless airplanes? — **A.** concerned, **B.** not concerned
....**A-B / NI-PC-DB**
➤ (How do you feel about where automation is headed? — How do you feel about a Vehicle Milage Travel Tax?)

708. SMOKING: What's your attitude toward smoking? ....
....**NI-PC-DB**
➤ (in public & public buildings — in your own home — outside — restaurants — bars — smoking areas — second hand smoke — apartment.buildings — ads targeted to teens — health-related lawsuits — responsibility — affect on insurance — effect on health — coverage & rates — cost — treatments)

709. WEALTH GAP: Does the wealth or income gap in our country concern you? ....**Y-N / NI-PC-DB**

710. WELFARE: What's your attitude toward welfare? ....
....**NI-PC-DB**
➤ (the unemployed — poor — disabled — impoverished — mental health issues — homelessness — undocumented immigrants & their children — cost)

711. WOKE: Are you familiar with the "woke" culture? ....
....**Y-N / NI-PC-DB**

23. TIME

Important! Please read.

TABLE OF CONTENTS — Page 5
23 Chapters Listed Alphabetically — 723 Main Questions —

Key words in each chapter are in alphabetical order for that chapter.

ANSWER CHOICES
Y-N (Yes No) — T-F (True False) — A-B-C (Multiple Choice)

NI (Non-Issue) — PC (Potential Conflict) — DB (Deal Breaker)

HOW TO ADDRESS THE QUESTIONS
Whether you're in a relationship or not, answer first for yourself, then ask yourself, how would you feel if your partner or a potential partner were to choose differently or the opposite? If reviewing with a partner and areas of disagreement arise, engage your sense of humor, remain calm, and discuss your differences civilly.

JUDGING AN ENTRY
Whatever you feel about an entry, be careful not to underestimate the value of what may appear to be a petty or trivial issue. You'd be surprised, or maybe not, at how little it can take to start an argument or reveal a major difference of opinion. A discussion of these minor issues can sometimes be quite revelatory..

RIGHT & WRONG
There are no absolutely right or wrong answers, just your subjective opinions expressed as a starting point for deliberation or discussion.

☆☆☆☆☆

— Time —

712. **ALLOCATION: In any typical week, how much time do you have just for yourself?** ....**NI-PC-DB**
➤ (How much time do you spend with, **e.g.,** your mate — your children — family — friends — community — work — church — having fun?)

713. **ALLOCATION: Percentage-wise, how much of your available free time do you imagine allocating to togetherness with a partner vs. personal alone time?**
....**NI-PC-DB**

714. **ALLOCATION: When competing for your time, who comes first — A. a BFF, B. family, C. spouse, D. your work boss, E. children, F. boy-girl friend?, G. clients & customers** ....**A-B-C-D-E-F / NI-PC-DB**
➤ (Would your answer change if a family member were ill? — Is your answer dependent on, **e.g.,** how long you've been married or dating — the age of your children — the closeness of your friend — your financial situation — the importance of your job?)

715. **ALLOCATION: Do you ever spend time truly doing nothing?** ....**Y-N / NI-PC-DB**
➤ (not reading — no TV — no radio — no music — not walking with headphones — not gardening — not talking — no cell phone activity — not even busy bathing — no external sensory input — just thinking in quiet — resting & relaxing — sunning — soaking in a hot tub, alone — meditating — watching the clouds drift by — enclosed in a sensory deprivation cocoon — totally immersed in your mind only — solitary confinement — Covid quarantine — no outside mental distractions)

716. **AMOUNT: What do people desire most — A. more time, B. more money?** ....**A-B / NI-PC-DB**

717. **AMOUNT: If given an extra hour a day, how would you spend it?** ....**NI-PC-DB**

— Time —

718. **AMOUNT: A lack of time is one of the most common complaints people have & one of the greatest causes of stress.** ....T-F / NI-PC-DB
➤ (Does your schedule have you under constant time pressure? — Are your time issues self or externally created?

719. **HEALER: Time heals all wounds.** ....T-F / NI-PC-DB

720. **IMPORTANCE: On a scale of 1 to 5 , how much of an issue or preoccupation is 'time' in your life, either as an individual or in a relationship?** ....1-2-3-4-5 / NI-PC-DB

721. **IMPORTANCE: Can you give a gift more valuable than your time or money?** ....Y-N / NI-PC-DB
➤ (How about your attention — love — caring — listening — inspiration —hope — other?)

722. **MANAGEMENT: Is time-management —** <u>**A.** a major problem, **B.** a minor problem, **C.** not a problem at all?</u> .....
....A-B-C / NI-PC-DB
➤ (Do you start a day by attacking the biggest, hardest tasks first, or by knocking off some easy ones, in order to check off some wins?)

723. **MISTAKES: Many of our mistakes & injuries occur when we're rushing or in a hurry due to time pressures & deadlines.** ....T-F / NI-PC-DB
➤ (What percent of the time do you feel rushed? — Is there a difference between weekdays & weekends?)

724. **Never: Never say never.** ....T-F / NI-PC-DB
➤ (What percent of the time do you feel rushed? — Is there a difference between weekdays & weekends?)

— Time —

725. **PERIOD: Which time period do you 'live in' or prefer to reflect on the most?** — **A.** the past, **B.** the present, **C.** the future ....A-B-C / NI-PC-DB
➤ (When engaged in self-reflection, which person within you makes you feel the best...the one you were — the one you are — the one you can be? — How do you envision your future? — Would you like to know your future, assuming it could be known? — What are your favorite or fondest memories?)

726. **PROBLEMS: Do you view your time problems as** — **A.** there's not enough hours in the day, **B.** too many demands on your time, **C.** difficulty saying no to impositions on your time, **D.** lack of time-management skills?..A-B-C-D / NI-PC-DB
➤ (Given that your days will never exceed more than 24 hours, isn't it a waste of time to say, "if only I had more time." — Which demands on your time are most troublesome: social & friends, business or financial, family, legal, medical, maintenance, other?

727. **SPEED: How do you feel about the passing of time?** — **A.** it's going too fast, it flies, **e.g.,** there are only 11 years between 29 & 40, **B.** too slow, it drags, **C.** it's passing just right ....A-B-C / NI-PC-DB
➤ (Does your answer depend on whether you're looking forward or backward? — Does your answer depend on your current state of mind, happy or not? — Are you in a hurry to get where you want to be? Are you pacing yourself, or do you often feel out of sync with life itself?)

To order additional books, see last page.

10-Secrets To A Long & Happy Marriage

1.   Luck and timing.

2.   Choose your mate wisely — fully aware of the cost of a poor choice: divorce, lost wealth, wasted time, impact on children and health, lost love, lost inspiration, etc.

3.   Develop a healthy tolerance for conflict, contentious disagreements, and heated debates. It can be entertainment for a spirited mind.

4.   Don't mind-read or expect your mind to be read. Communicate! *"Don't want to talk about it"* solves nothing and should be 'off-the-table.'

5.   Next to fidelity, loyalty, and love, trust is paramount. Develop it daily by living up to your word.

6.   Defend publicly, chastise privately.

7.   Patience and persistence. A successful and fulfilling marriage takes work; it doesn't happen by accident.

8.   Seek to understand before demanding to be understood.

9.   Forgiveness, but only if the offender confesses, expresses genuine remorse, and is sincerely repentant.

10. Before you commit to a relationship…TALK, TALK, and TALK…about everything; your likes and dislikes; what you can and can't tolerate; your loves and hates. Share things about yourself that might be embarrassing or against your self-interest. Doing so elicits trust and honesty from your partner. Good luck!

30 Great Quotations

The following **30** quotations out of **8,540** in our book entitled *Quotations To Help You — From Out of Their Minds* represent 547 quotations on **Love**, **Marriage**, **Relationships**, **Friends** and **Friendship.**

These 8,540 quotations, collected over the past 47 years, by yours truly, are indexed and cross-referenced under 1,500 key words.

Based on book-owner testimonials, we consider our quotations book *"the most extraordinarily useful and useable book of quotations that you and your mind could ever benefit from."*

To see a video presentation on our book, visit our website, **TheThinkingPlace.Com** and click on **Quotation Book** in the navigation bar at the top of the page.

1.   "Immature love says, I love you because I need you. Mature love says I need you because I love you." — *Erich Fromm*

2.   "Love and humor are the soul's weapons in the fight for self-preservation." — *Dr. Viktor E. Frankl*

3.   "When the satisfaction or the security of another person becomes as significant to one as one's own satisfaction or security, then the state of love exists." — *Henry Stack Sullivan*

4.   "Man needs very little if he knows the transforming joy of human love." — *Everett L. Shostrom & James Kavanaugh*

5.   "If you cannot inspire a woman with love of you, fill her above the brim with love of herself; all that runs over will be yours." —   *C(harles) C(aleb) Colton*

6.   "In the eyes of a lover pockmarks are dimples." — *Proverb-Japanese*

7.   "You can bear your own faults, and why not a fault in your wife?" — *Benjamin Franklin*

8.   "Keep your eyes wide open before marriage, half shut afterwards." — *Benjamin Franklin*

9.   "A good marriage is the union of two forgivers." — *Ruth Bell Graham*

— Quotations —

10. "If there is such a thing as a good marriage, it is because it resembles friendship rather than love." — *Michel de Montaigne*

11. "When a man opens the car door for his wife, it's either a new car or a new wife." — *Prince Philip*

12. "No matter how happily a woman may be married, it always pleases her to discover that there is a nice man who wishes she were not." — *H(enry) L(ouis) Mencken*

13. "Nothing flatters a man as much as the happiness of his wife; he is always proud of himself as the source of it." — *Dr. Samuel Johnson*

14. "It doesn't much matter whom one marries, for one is sure to find next morning that it was someone else." — *Samuel Rogers*

15. "He who burns his bridges better be a damn good swimmer." — *Harvey Mackay*

16. "Almost all of our relationships begin, and most of them continue, as forms of mutual exploitation, a mental or physical barter, to be terminated when one or both parties run out of goods." — *W(ystan) H(ugh) Auden*

17. "It's not who you know, it's how you are known by those who know you." — *Gene Autry*

18. "If you think you've got someone eating out of your hand, it's a good idea to count your fingers." — *Martin Bushbaum*

19. "Don't tell your friends their social faults: they will cure the fault and never forgive you." — *Logan Pearsall Smith*

20. "It is well, when one is judging a friend, to remember that he is judging you with the same godlike and superior impartiality." — *Arnold Bennett*

21. "Chance makes our parents, but choice makes our friends." — *Jacques Delille*

22. "Woe to him that is alone when he falleth; for he hath not another to help him up." — *Bible / Ecclesiastes 4-10*

23. "One friend in a lifetime is much; two are many; three are hardly possible." — *Henry Brooks Adams*

— *Quotations* —

24. "A friend is one who has the same enemies you have." — ***Abraham Lincoln***

25. "A friend is a person with whom I may be sincere; before him I may think aloud." — ***Ralph Waldo Emerson***

26. "Friendship often ends in love; but love in friendship never." — ***C(harles) C(aleb) Colton***

27. "Friendship is feeling safe with another person, having neither to weigh thoughts nor measure words." — ***Rex Cole***

28. "Few friendships would endure if each party knew what his friend said about him in his absence, even when speaking sincerely and dispassionately." — ***Blaise Pascal***

29. "Friendship is love minus sex and plus reason. Love is friendship plus sex and minus reason." — ***Mason Cooley***

30. "What greater thing is there for two human souls than to feel that they are joined for life to strengthen each other in all labor, to rest on each other in all sorrow, to minister to each other in all pain." — ***George Eliot (Marian Evans Cross)***

Testimonials

Alex E. — Marriage and Family Therapist

- I love this book!

- Have you ever committed to a relationship you would have been better off without, or stayed in a relationship too long, unable to decide if you should stay or go? If so, this book can help you avoid making the same mistakes over again by helping you figure out what is best for you, so you can avoid spending years, possibly even decades involved in an unfulfilling relationship.

- Even If you just want to get to know yourself and your partner better, be kind to yourself and check it out. It is an easy read and a great conversation starter.

- The book is extremely organized and comprehensive and covers so many important issues people fail to discuss when they first "fall in love." It will not only help you define your own values, it will help you think about and discover the values you need your life partner to posses, as well.

- This book will be so beneficial to the couples in my practice by helping them achieve clarity in their relationships. Whether they choose to remain together or not, they will gain a better understanding of themselves and their needs.

- Groundbreaking book!

Barbara S. — Real Estate Broker

- This book about relationships is the most comprehensive guide to uncovering potential partnership issues due to differences in values, goals, needs or desires.

- Use this checklist to help you avoid the pitfalls that come with making poor relationship choices.

- Make it fun but get to the real issues of your potential partner's personality, and then decide, using the adult part of your brain, if you have enough in common to be in a fulfilling relationship, instead of discovering months or years later that you never really knew what you were getting into.

Bill L. — Retired Photographer

- Profoundly comprehensive. See your life in a new light.

— Testimonials —

Dolby D. — Board Certified Personal Coach

- What an insightful, almost genius idea to create a book to get people to think about critical information before embracing genuinely into relationships of any kind.

- Allows one to get to know themselves better. If you do not know you, how will you be able to be fully present to another.

- A terrific party book. A winner.

Gabriela S. — Mother of Two Sons

- A must read.

- Great compilation of topics for discussion with your potential soulmate.

- Helps you become more aware of things you can do before you take the plunge.

- Can also assist you to bring your relationships to a higher level, especially the relationship with yourself.

- Makes for a great gift. I recently purchased a few that I gave away to family members, friends and relatives. They expressed how it quickly became a source of reference.

- Wish I knew how to address a variety of these issues before I got married over 20 years ago.

Geno A. — Author & Caregiver

- Fun, thought-provoking conversation piece for a casual gathering.

- Comprehensive study of people and personal preferences.

Karen M. — Mother of Three Sons

- Loved it so much I gifted it for my college-aged son, his girlfriend, other loved ones, and some close friends, as well.

- Best investment in me I've ever made.

Leslie R. — Sustainable Living Advocate

- Thought provoking.

- Prompted insightful conversations between us, helping us to find out how compatible we really are.

- Conversations over dinner resulted in livelier conversations than talking about the weather or our schedules. Recommend it highly!

Maddy P. — Executive Sales Manager

- How many times have you heard someone say that when we're born, we don't come with an instruction manual? I've heard it a gazillion times. Though the **Relationship Compatibility Checklist** is not an instruction manual, it is the perfect guide for getting the information you need when making decisions in (and for) your life.

- Should be on everyone's gift list.

- Every dating site, therapist, or life coach needs to give this book to their clients.

Madison G. — Notary & Student

- A collection of carefully thought-out questions and scenarios that force you to be honest with yourself and what you need in your life.

- Allows you to make thoughtful, mature decisions about certain situations before they even happen so you'll know your stance when they do. it.

Margaret P. — Social Security Administrator

- Showed this book to my boyfriend and it helped me to have an open conversation about many controversial issues. Helped to clarify where we stand in our relationship and what our next step may be.

Mary S. — Retiree

- A wonderful book. Informative, educational, enlightening, even transformative. Doesn't tell you how to think, only what to think about. I loved this book.

Mounia B. — Termite Inspector

- I love this book.

Pete W. — Divorce Mediator

- While the book is certainly helpful for folks thinking about getting married, it can also benefit those in long term relationships, as well.

- Non-technical, simple, and easy to use. Highly recommend this book. A tool for professionals to use when working with clients.

Raeesa H. — Fundraiser

- Really useful in finding connections with your partner that you didn't even realize were there. Fun to question things we often take for granted. Highly recommend!

— Testimonials —

Richard B. — Real Estate Investor
- Discover the ongoing benefits of in-depth conversations with current and, or potential relationships!

Ron W. — Manufacturer
- I love your new book.

Russell W. — Portrait Painter Artist
- A must have for all potential relationships and even helpful during a current one.

Sandy D. — CPA
- A very comprehensive tool, but an easy and fun read. A must for any relationship, even a successful one. Makes you realize what's really important in life.

Sharon J. — Home Health Caregiver
- My partner of 6 years and I have been considering taking our relationship to the next level of commitment. Now there is no doubt that we were made for one another. We hear wedding bells!!

Stephen B. — Actor
- A great book.

- I'm a single guy. This book will no doubt greatly increase my chances of finding the compatible woman of my dreams.

Tobey D. — Wedding Consultant
- The questions, by opening up communication avenues, in a non-threatening way, can help couples understand each others feelings.

- Determine whether that person is a keeper or not.

Tom Z. — Author
- I don't believe the Amazon blurb does this gem justice.

- Perhaps the finest list ever complied to help people understand how they truly feel and think. Can help the reader discern whether the relationship they are in, or pondering, is the real deal or merely window dressing.

- Non-preachy and chock full of wisdom. Allows an open minded person to go into a relationship with eyes wide open. Ought to be required reading before any marriage license is granted. 5 Stars.

How to Order Additional Books:

A Great Gift Item!

Your purchase also includes *The Thinkers Edge*, a periodic email comprised of motivational, thought-provoking content.

To order

1. Go to **Amazon.Com**

2. Search *Relationship Compatibility Checklist* or under *Mel Solon*

Or

- Amazon/Kindle
- Apple iBooks
- eBay
- Book stores near you.
- For more information — Call **Mel** at **818.222.4477**

See YouTube video
Relationship Compatibility Checklist

Publisher: Why Not? Publications
Author Publisher: Mel Solon

Learn the most important worth knowing about interpersonal relationship compatibility.

Please share. Help fix the couple and fix the world as a byproduct.

Made in the USA
Las Vegas, NV
24 October 2021

33014335R00105